When You Need a Bible Story

When You Need a
BIBLE STORY

by

ELIZABETH B. JONES

BEACON HILL PRESS
Kansas City, Missouri

PRINTED IN THE UNITED STATES OF AMERICA

To my daughter

BETTY JONES TAYLOR

whose invaluable help has made
this book possible

Contents

II. GOD SO LOVED THE WORLD

Stories of Jesus and His Friends

I

Long, Long Ago

Stories from the
Old Testament

When God Made the World

Long, long ago there was no beautiful green earth. There was no sun to give warmth and light. There was no moon nor stars to shine by night. There were only water and darkness everywhere.

But there was God. Always there was God. Then God said, "Let there be light," and there was light. God divided the light from the darkness. The light He called *Day*, and the darkness *Night*.

Next God made the firmament (the sky) and divided the firmament from the waters below.

"The firmament shall be called heaven," He said.

Then God gathered the waters together in one place and said, "Let the dry land appear." God called the dry land *Earth*, and the waters he called *Seas*.

After this God made the sun to give light by day, and the moon and stars to give light by night.

God made the rivers, and the oceans. He made the tall, tall mountains and the valleys in between. He made the grass to grow and the trees to put forth their leaves.

Then God made living creatures. He made the fish to swim in the waters. He made the birds to fly through the air. He made all the creatures large and small that crawl or walk on the earth.

What a wonderful world it was that God had made But God was not through with His work yet.

"Let Us make man like Us," God said. So God made the very first man. God made man to be like Him. Man could think and love. He could choose between right and wrong. The first man was called Adam.

Then God said to Adam, "I have given you this

world to enjoy. I will give you every plant and every tree. I will give you all the fish in the water. I will give you every animal and every living thing that I have made. You may take care of this world and use all these good things for your own good."

Adam was glad for the beautiful world that God had given him.

"I will give everything a name," said Adam. So he named all the animals and every living thing that came before him.

God had given Adam a wonderful world, but still there was something missing. Adam was all alone in the world. There was no one for him to talk to. There was no one to enjoy with him the beautiful flowers and the trees, or listen to the birds. There was no one to help him do the work that God had given him to do.

"I am lonely," said Adam. "I need someone to talk to. I need someone to help me."

"It is not good for you to live alone," God said to Adam. "I will make a helper for you."

So God made a beautiful woman named Eve. How happy Adam was now!

"Eve shall be my wife," Adam said. "Ours will be the very first family in the beautiful world that God has made."

So Adam and Eve lived together in a beautiful garden called Eden. They were very happy together as God had planned.

But the time came when Adam and Eve disobeyed God. They chose to do wrong instead of right. Then sin came into the world. Sin means disobeying God. Sin means separation from God. So Adam and Eve had to leave the beautiful garden.

They went far away from God. But God did not stop loving them. Even then God had a loving plan to save people from their sins, and to bring them back to Him.

A Faithful Man Obeys God

It had now been a long, long time since Adam and Eve had lived in the garden. Now there were many, many people on the earth. These people did not love God. They did not try to serve Him. Their hearts were full of sin and they did many wicked things. What a sad, wicked world it was!

God was very sad as He looked at the beautiful world He had made!

"I am sorry I made the world," He said. "I am sorry I made man, for everyone on earth is wicked except Noah."

Noah was a man who loved God and wanted to obey Him. Noah did not do the wicked things that other people did.

One day God spoke to Noah and said: "There is going to be a great flood, Noah. The whole earth will be destroyed because of sin and wickedness. But I will save you and your family if you will obey Me."

"I will obey you," Noah answered. "What do You want me to do?"

"I want you to build a great ark [that is a ship]. There will be room in it for you and your family. There will be room for two of every living creature on the earth."

Then God told Noah just how to make the ark.

"I will get busy at once," Noah said, "and my sons will help me too."

What a busy time Noah and his sons had building the big ark! *Saw, saw, saw,* went the saws as they cut the gopher wood. *Bang, bang, bang,* went the hammers as they nailed the boards together.

When Noah's neighbors saw what he was doing, they made fun of him.

"Look what Noah is doing," they said, laughing. "He is building a big ship he calls an ark. But where is the water for such a big ship? It is on dry land!"

"Ha, ha, ha," they laughed. "Noah is crazy and so are his sons."

But Noah paid no attention to them. He and his sons went on building the ark. After many years it was all finished. It had been made just as God had said to build it. It was three stories high and 450 feet long. It was made of gopher wood and covered inside and out with pitch so it wouldn't leak. What a fine ship it was!

Then God said, "Come, Noah, bring your family and two of all the living things into the ark. In seven days the rain will start and then the flood will come."

Noah obeyed God at once. Soon he and his family were safely in the ark. Then two by two went all the animals and all the other living creatures just as God had said. There was plenty of food and water. Then God shut the door and they were safe inside.

Then the rain began. Oh, how it rained, for forty days and forty nights! Soon there was water, water everywhere.

The ark rose higher and higher with the flood until at last it drifted away on top of the water.

For six months the ark floated around on the water. When the water began to go down again, the ark came to rest on a high mountain.

All this time Noah and his family were safe and happy inside. How glad they were that Noah had obeyed God and had built the ark! How glad they were that God had saved them from the terrible flood!

God Makes a Promise

Noah and his family had been in the ark for a long, long time. At first the ark had floated on the water. Then it had come to rest on the top of a mountain.

The rains were over now and the water was slowly going down.

"When can we leave the ark?" Noah's family wanted to know.

"As soon as the water has gone and the earth is dry enough," Noah told them.

"When will that be?" they wondered.

"Look," said Noah, opening the window which was on the top of the ark. "See those mountaintops around us? The water is dropping all the time!"

Then one day he opened the window and let out a dove.

"The dove will let us know if the water is all gone," Noah told his family.

But it wasn't long until the dove came back. Noah opened the window and took her back into the ark.

"That proves that water is still covering the trees" Noah said, "for she found no place to light."

He waited another seven days and then opened the window of the ark and let out the dove again. That evening the dove came back again. But this time she had a green olive leaf in her mouth.

"Oh," cried Noah's family, "the water has dropped below the trees! Let's leave the ark now."

But Noah shook his head. "We will wait a little longer," he said.

15

In seven more days Noah let the dove out again. He waited and waited. But the dove did not come back.

"The earth will soon be dry again," he said happily.

It was not many weeks until God spoke to Noah and said, "Come out of the ark now, Noah. Bring your family and all the animals and other living things."

So Noah and his family left the ark and walked out onto the land once more. Oh, how good it seemed to leave the ark where they had been so long! How sweet and fresh the air seemed! How beautiful and clean the world about them looked!

"God has been very good to us," Noah said to his family. "He has saved us from the terrible flood. He has given us this beautiful, clean world to live in and to care for."

"First of all, we will build an altar and worship Him."

So Noah built an altar and knelt down to worship God.

"Thank You, God," he said, "for helping me to build the ark. Thank You for taking care of us through the long months in the ark. Thank You for food to eat and water to drink.

"Thank You now for this beautiful, clean world to live in."

God was pleased with Noah's "thank-you" prayer. He was pleased with the way Noah had obeyed Him. Then God made Noah a wonderful promise.

"Never again will the earth be destroyed with water," God said. "While the earth remains, there will always be seedtime and harvest, cold and heat, summer and winter, and day and night.

"See the rainbow in the sky, Noah? When you see this bow, remember My promise to you and to all who live on the earth."

An Important Choice

Pad, pad, pad, went the tired feet of the camels. *Tinkle, tinkle, tinkle,* went the little bells around their necks.

Eliezer sat up on one of the tall camels and looked across the burning sand.

"I see the city of Nahor at last," he said wearily.

Eliezer was a servant of the rich man Abraham. He had come all the way to the city of Nahor to find a wife for Abraham's son Isaac.

"Go back to the land where I used to live," Abraham had told him. "There you will find a good wife for Isaac."

Eliezer was glad to do as Abraham had said. But now as he came near to the city of Nahor, he wondered just what to do. "How will I know whom to choose?" he said to himself.

Just outside the city of Nahor was a big well. All the people of the city came there for water.

"I am so tired and thirsty," said Eliezer. "My camels are tired and thirsty too. We will rest here by the well until someone comes to draw water for us."

As Eliezer rested there by the well, he thought, "All the young women of the city come here for water. This will be a good place to choose a wife for Isaac."

Then Eliezer prayed: "O God, help me to find the right wife for Isaac. If I ask a young woman for a drink of water, and she offers to give water to my camels also, let this be the way I will know which is the right one."

Soon Eliezer heard footsteps. He looked up to see

17

a beautiful young woman named Rebekah coming to the well for water.

Eliezer watched Rebekah draw water from the well. Then he said, "Will you give me a drink?"

"Of course," said Rebekah kindly. She held the water pitcher up so Eliezer could take a good, cool drink. Then she said, "Your camels are hot and thirsty too. I will draw water for them also."

As Eliezer watched Rebekah draw water for the camels, he thought, "This is the one God wants me to choose as Isaac's wife."

Then he said to Rebekah, "Do you have a place at your home where I could stay all night?"

"Yes," said Rebekah. "Come home with me."

When Eliezer and Rebekah reached her home, her family was very kind to him also.

"I must tell you why I have come," said Eliezer. "My master, Abraham, has sent me to find a wife for his son Isaac. I want to choose Rebekah. Will you let me take her back with me?"

"We will let Rebekah decide," said her family.

"Yes, I will go," said Rebekah.

The very next day Rebekah started back with Eliezer. *Pad, pad, pad,* went the feet of the camels, all the way over the hot, dusty sand until they came to Abraham's home.

As soon as Isaac saw Rebekah, he loved her. They were married very soon.

How glad Eliezer was that God had helped him to choose the right wife for Isaac!

Jacob Has a Dream

Isaac and Rebekah were very proud of their twin sons. But the boys were not at all alike. Esau loved to hunt in the wilds. He was a good hunter. Jacob tended the sheep and helped around the house.

Isaac had taught his sons about God. He had taught them to love and serve God as he did. But Jacob was a selfish young man who wanted everything for himself. He did not like it because Esau, who had been born first, would receive a double portion of their father's wealth.

"I must have Esau's birthright," Jacob said to himself. So he schemed and schemed how to get it. One day when Esau came home from a hunting trip tired and hungry, Jacob offered to trade him a good meal for his birthright. It was a bad trade, but Esau did not think about that. He only thought of what he wanted right then. So he made the trade.

As the elder son, Esau was to receive a special blessing from his father, and Jacob wanted that too.

One day Isaac said to his son Esau, "Go out into the woods and hunt some venison to cook for me. When I have eaten it, I will give you my special blessing."

This special blessing was like a prayer, asking God to be with the person who received it.

"How can I get Father's special blessing?" Jacob wondered. "Esau does not care about it. He only cares for hunting and eating. He traded me his birthright. Why should he want the blessing?"

Jacob's mother thought Jacob should have the special blessing. She dressed Jacob up in Esau's clothes and put goatskins on his hands and arms to make them hairy like Esau's. Then she cooked some delicious meat for Jacob to take to Isaac.

Now Isaac was very, very old and blind. He could not see Jacob at all.

"Your voice sounds like Jacob's," said Isaac. He reached out and felt Jacob's hands. They felt like Esau's. He smelled the outdoor smell on Esau's clothes that Jacob was wearing.

"You must be Esau," Isaac said. "Let me eat the good food and then I will bless you."

So Jacob received the blessing that Isaac meant to give Esau. When Esau came home from his hunting trip, oh, how angry he was! Jacob knew he must leave home at once, for there was no telling what his brother might do to him.

"Go to my brother's home," his mother said. That was a long, long journey away.

Jacob ran out into the wilderness country as fast as he could go. He walked and walked over the hot sands toward his uncle's home.

When nighttime came, Jacob needed rest. But there was no nice, soft bed for Jacob that night. He gathered together a few stones for a pillow and wrapped his robe around him.

The night was dark and still. All alone there in the darkness Jacob was afraid. He thought of the wrong things he had done. He looked up at the stars and thought about God. Did God love him in spite of the wrong things he had done? Would God forgive him? Jacob didn't know, but he felt very, very sad and sorry for what he had done.

At last Jacob fell asleep and began to dream. In his dream he saw a ladder that reached up to heaven. There on the ladder were angels from heaven going up and down. Then Jacob heard God speak to him. "I am the Lord God of Abraham and Isaac. I am with you, Jacob, and will keep you in all places wherever you go. I will not leave you."

When Jacob awoke he said, "Surely God was in this place and I did not know it."

Then Jacob took the stones he had used for a pillow and poured oil on them. This meant it was a very special place because God had spoken to him.

"The Lord shall be my God," said Jacob. "Of all the Lord gives to me I will surely give a tenth to Him."

From Slave to Ruler

Jacob had twelve sons, whom he loved very much. He was good to all his sons, and especially good to Joseph. Or at least that is what Joseph's brothers thought. They were jealous of Joseph.

"Joseph is our father's favorite," they would say. "See the beautiful coat he made for Joseph? See how he listens to Joseph's silly dreams?"

Joseph did have strange dreams. He dreamed once that his father and brothers bowed down before him. These dreams made his brothers angrier than ever. "We will never bow down to him," they said.

One day when Joseph's brothers were far away tending their sheep, Jacob called Joseph to him. "Go and find your brothers," he said. "I want to know how they are getting along."

So Joseph started out to find his brothers. It was a long, long walk but at last he found them tending their sheep.

The brothers saw Joseph coming. "Here comes that silly dreamer," they said. "Let's get rid of him."

They took Joseph and put him in a deep hole. A little while later they saw a caravan coming across the desert.

"These are traders going to Egypt," they said. "Let's sell Joseph to them as a slave."

So poor Joseph was taken out of the hole and sold to the traders.

"We will take his coat home to Father," they said, "and he will think wild animals have killed Joseph."

The brothers went home to tell their father the sad news. Meanwhile Joseph was taken far away by the traders. Day after day he traveled with the camel train all the way to Egypt.

Joseph was very glad when the camel train stopped at last. He was very hot and tired. He was sad and lonely too when he thought about his home.

"I wonder what my father thought when I did not come home again," he said to himself.

Although Joseph was sad, he was not afraid. He knew that God would be with him in this strange country.

There in Egypt, Joseph was sold to an officer in the king's army named Potiphar. Potiphar liked Joseph very much. "You are a good worker, Joseph," Potiphar often said. Then one day he put Joseph in charge of his house.

But Potiphar's wife became angry with Joseph and told her husband that Joseph had done something wrong. This was not true but Joseph was put in prison anyway. While in prison he worked hard and soon was put in charge of other prisoners.

"Joseph is good to us," the prisoners said. "He can even tell us the meaning of our dreams."

Then one day the king of Egypt had some strange dreams. "What do my dreams mean?" he wondered.

One of the king's helpers had been in prison with

Joseph. "Joseph can tell you what your dreams mean," he told the king.

So the king sent for Joseph and told him his strange dreams. "Tell me what they mean," the king said.

"I can't tell you, but God will help me to tell you," said Joseph.

God helped Joseph to know the meaning of the king's dream.

"There will be seven years of good crops and plenty of food in Egypt," Joseph told the king. "Then there will be seven bad years. You must save food during the seven good years, so you will be prepared for the bad ones."

"I will do as you say," said the king, "and, Joseph, I will make you my special helper. You will be a ruler in Egypt and will be in charge of gathering food during the good years."

"God will be with me," said Joseph. "He will help me to be a good ruler."

So Joseph became the king's special helper. God helped him to be a very good helper and he was able to store up enough food for all the bad years in Egypt.

Corn in Egypt

Jacob and his family were in trouble. There had been no rain in all the land of Israel. The crops dried up. The grass stopped growing. And now there was no grain for food.

"There is grain in the land of Egypt," said Jacob to his sons. "You must go there and buy some. But Benjamin, my youngest son, must stay home with me."

While Benjamin stayed home with Jacob, the other ten sons started out on the long trip to Egypt.

The men traveled day after day through the dry, thirsty land toward Egypt. As they went along they thought about their brother Joseph.

"This is probably the very road Joseph travelled along with the Ishmaelites we sold him to," said Simeon sadly.

"Yes," said Judah, "poor Joseph must be dead now. How could we have done such a terrible thing?"

"What would our father say if he knew what we did?" said Levi.

The brothers talked sadly about Joseph all the way to Egypt. They did not know what would happen when they reached there.

Everyone who came to Egypt to buy grain had to talk to Joseph first. So the brothers came and bowed down before him. They did not know it was their brother, but Joseph knew them. He was so glad to see them again that he turned his head and cried.

Then he said, "Is your father alive? And do you have another brother?"

"Our father is alive," they said, "and we have another brother named Benjamin."

"The next time you come bring Benjamin with you," said Joseph. "I will keep one of you here until you return."

So Simeon had to stay in Egypt while the other brothers went sadly home.

When their father, Jacob, heard what had happened, he said, "I will never let Benjamin go to Egypt!" But soon the grain was all gone, and the brothers had to go back to Egypt for more. There was nothing to do but to take Benjamin with them.

Joseph was glad to see his brothers again. He was glad to see Benjamin too. "I must find out if my brothers are really sorry," he said to himself. When

24

the brothers started home this time, Joseph sent a servant after them. "Benjamin must stay in Egypt," the servant said.

Sadly the brothers went back to see Joseph.

"Oh, don't keep Benjamin here," they said. "Our father would die if he didn't return." And then Judah said, "Let me stay in his place."

Now Joseph knew his brothers were really sorry for what they had done to him.

He began to cry. "Don't you know I am your brother Joseph?" he said.

How surprised the brothers were! They were a-fraid, too, for they were now at his mercy.

"I have forgiven you," Joseph told them. "Now I want you and my father to come to Egypt to live with me so that I may take care of you until the famine is over."

Joseph gave many fine gifts to his brothers. He gave each one new clothes to wear, and food to eat on the way home. He gave them wagons and donkeys laden with fine gifts for his father also.

When Jacob heard the good news about Joseph, he could hardly believe it. "It can't be true," he said sadly.

"But it is true, Father," said his sons. "See the fine things Joseph has sent you? He wants you to come to Egypt to see him. He wants all of us to live with him there."

Then Jacob believed the good news. "I will go and see my son," he said.

But Jacob was now an old man. It was a long, long trip to Egypt. Jacob needed to know that God would be with him.

That night God spoke to Jacob. "Jacob, Jacob," God said, "don't be afraid to go down to Egypt. I will go with you and will make of you a great nation."

So Jacob and all his family packed their things and started for Egypt. They took their wagons and oxen with them. They took their sheep and cattle. At last they came to the border of Egypt. Jacob sent word to Joseph that he was coming. Joseph jumped into a chariot and came as fast as he could to meet his father.

"Father, Father!" he cried as he hugged his father.

"O my son!" cried Jacob.

What a happy time it was!

Jacob settled down with his family in Egypt. Joseph was glad to take care of his father and all his brothers and their families.

A Secret Hiding Place

"Sh-h-h-h," said Miriam as she patted her baby brother. "Don't cry or someone will hear you."

Mother was busy making a basket bed for the little one. It was shaped like a boat and covered with pitch on the outside to make it float in water.

"Little Brother will be safe and snug in here," said Mother as she tucked in some warm, soft blankets.

"Will God take care of our baby in there?" Miriam wanted to know.

"I am sure He will," said Mother. "He will not let the wicked king find our baby."

Cold shivers went over Miriam as she thought about the king. He wanted to kill all Hebrew boy babies. That was why her little brother needed a good hiding place. That was why Mother had made the strange little boat bed.

"He is asleep now," Miriam said.

"That is good," said Mother, "I will put him in his new bed while he is asleep."

Mother lifted the baby in her arms and kissed him gently on the cheek. Then she tucked him in the little bed. Down the path the three went toward the river.

When they reached the riverbank, Mother stooped down and placed the bed into the water. There it was safely hidden among the tall reeds.

"I want you to hide nearby and watch," Mother said to Miriam. "Be sure to call me if anything happens."

Miriam hid in the weeds along the riverbank. She sat there as quiet as a little mouse until suddenly she heard footsteps. Then she peeked out to see who was coming. Why, it was the king's daughter, the princess, and her maids, coming to bathe in the river! Oh, what would happen now?

Miriam held her breath as she watched the princess walk along the riverbank. Then she heard her say:

"Look at that tiny boat there in the bulrushes. Bring it to me at once."

Miriam watched as the maids brought the little boat up out of the water and put it down in front of the princess. The princess stooped over and looked inside.

"Oh, oh," she cried, "what a beautiful little baby!"

The baby was awake now and he began to cry. The princess picked him up gently out of his little bed and held him in her arms. "This must be a little Hebrew boy," she said softly. "What can I do to keep him safe?"

Just then Miriam came out of her hiding place and stood near the princess.

"Shall I find you a nurse for the baby?" she asked.

"Yes," said the princess, "Please do."

Miriam ran up the path toward home as fast as she could go.

"Mother, Mother," she cried, "the princess has found

27

my little brother," and wants somebody to look after him for her. You could be his nurse. Come."

Mother came as fast as she could and bowed before the princess.

"Take care of this baby for me," said the princess. "I will call him Moses because I found him in the water."

Mother and Miriam were very glad to take little Moses home again. They would not need to hide him anymore. They were glad that God had helped them. And they spent many happy days caring for the little baby Moses.

Escape in the Night

"Taa-ho-o-o-o-o." That was Moses calling his sheep.

When the sheep heard Moses calling, they began to follow at once. Moses led them to the foot of a tall mountain. Then he sat down to rest while the sheep slowly wandered about, nibbling the tender grass.

As Moses sat there, he looked up at the beautiful mountains. He looked around at the bushes and the desert flowers.

"What a beautiful world God has made!" Moses said to himself.

Moses often thought about God while he was tending his sheep. He remembered what his mother had taught him when he was a boy.

As Moses thought about God, he also thought about his people. The Egyptians were making life hard for the Israelites. They were nothing more than slaves. Though Moses had been brought up in the palace, he had tried to help his people.

One day he saw some of them being beaten by the Egyptians and in anger he killed one of the guards. Then Moses escaped into this shepherd country. But he did not forget his people back in Egypt.

As Moses sat there that day watching his sheep, suddenly something strange happened.

There in front of him was a burning bush. The fire seemed to come right out of the middle of the bush but the bush itself was not burned up.

"I must see what is happening here," said Moses. But as he went nearer to the bush a Voice called out, "Moses, Moses."

"Here I am," said Moses, more surprised than ever.

"Do not come near the bush," the Voice said. "This is a holy place. Take off your shoes, for I am God, whom Isaac and Jacob worshiped."

Then God said, "I know all the trouble My people are having in Egypt. I know how cruelly they are being treated by the Egyptians. Moses, I want you to go back to Egypt and help them. I want you to ask the king to let My people leave Egypt and go back to the good land of their forefathers—the land I gave to Abraham."

"Oh," cried Moses. "I can't do that! That is too hard for me."

"I will be with you and help you," God said.

"But what shall I tell the people?" Moses asked.

"Tell them that God sent you to lead them out of Egypt," God answered.

"But I can't even talk very well," said Moses. "I talk so slowly and I stutter too."

"I will help you," God told Moses. "And I will tell your brother, Aaron, to help too."

Moses could not understand all that God wanted him to do. He did not think that he could do it by himself. But God had promised to go with him and help him.

"I will do what You ask," Moses said. "I will go back to Egypt and help my people."

The Hebrew people had lived in Egypt for a long, long time. They had been slaves so long they did not know what it would be like to be free. They were surprised when Moses came back and told them God wanted them to leave Egypt.

"How can we leave Egypt?" they said. "The king will not let us go."

"God wants me to talk to the king," said Moses.

Moses went to see the king and told him what God had said. But the king was very angry. "Your people can't go," he said.

Moses did not give up. He talked to the king many, many times. He talked to the Hebrew people too. God sent many troubles upon the Egyptian people, but still the king would not let the people leave.

Then one day God had something very important to tell Moses.

"Tell my people to get ready to leave Egypt tonight," God said. "Tell the fathers to bring in all the sheep and cattle. Tell the mothers to prepare food for a special midnight supper.

"When midnight comes, remember My words while you eat the special food. Do not sit down to eat. You must be ready to leave at once when the time comes."

Then God said, "A great trouble is coming to Egypt tonight. But I will help My people if they will obey Me."

When Moses told the people what God had said, they were very excited. They began at once to do as God said. The fathers brought in all the sheep and cattle. The mothers prepared food for the special supper. The boys and girls helped too in every way they could.

When the sun went down that night, everything was ready. The sheep and cattle were gathered together. The food was ready and all their belongings were packed.

When midnight came, the Egyptians were all sleeping as usual. But the Hebrew people were watching and eating the special supper as God had told them to do.

Then something happened! A cry went out through all the land of Egypt. A great trouble such as never had been known came to the land of Egypt. The oldest boy in every Egyptian family died, even the king's own son. Oh, what a sad time it was!

"Oh, oh," cried the king, "send Moses to me at once!"

Moses went to see the king in the middle of the night.

"Get your people up and leave Egypt tonight," said the king. "Take everything with you. Do not even wait until morning!"

Moses hurried from the king's palace to tell his people what the king had said.

"We must leave at once," he said, "before the king can change his mind."

The people were all ready. They quickly spread the word around and started at once. What a strange sight it must have been as the Hebrew people left Egypt!

There were six hundred thousand men, women, and children. They took with them all their sheep and cattle and everything else they had. They took silver and gold that the Egyptians had given them. They even took special bread to bake along the way. What an exciting time it was!

Moses was very glad for the way that God had helped him and his people. The Hebrew people were glad too. They did not know all that would happen to them, but they trusted God to take care of them as they journeyed back to their own land.

A Fearless Farmer

Swish, swish, swish. That was Gideon, the farmer's son, threshing out grain on the floor. Swish, swish, swish, went his rod on the pile of wheat.

Gideon was working as quietly as he could near a big cave.

"I must get this wheat threshed out and hide it in the cave before the Midianites come," he said to himself.

The Midianites were enemies of the Israelites. They came into their country and took away their homes. They stole their fruit and grain. The Israelites had to live in caves and try to hide away as much food as they could.

Swish, swish, swish, went Gideon's rod. Then suddenly he looked up and saw a stranger sitting under an oak tree nearby. Who could it be?

The stranger spoke to Gideon. "You are a brave man, Gideon. God is with you."

"Oh," said Gideon, "why do you say that? God has forgotten His people."

"God has not forgotten His people," said the stranger. "They have forgotten Him. But God wants to save His people from the Midianites."

Then Gideon knew that it was an angel speaking to him. He was afraid.

"Don't be afraid," said the angel. "God will help you."

When the angel had gone, Gideon built an altar and worshipped God. He called the altar "Peace." And that night he and some of his friends tore down the heathen idols which the Israelites had been worshipping.

"We will worship the true God," said Gideon.

Then God spoke to Gideon and told him all that He wanted him to do.

"Call your men together," God said.

So Gideon stood up bravely and blew on his trumpet. The men gathered quickly until there were 20,000 ready to fight the Midianites.

"You do not need all these men," God told Gideon. Then He told him how to choose the bravest of the men.

When Gideon had chosen the bravest, there were only 300 left to fight the Midianites.

"I will be with you, Gideon," God reassured him. Then God told him what He wanted him to do next.

When nighttime came the plan was all ready. Gideon gave each of his men a trumpet to blow and a pitcher with a torch inside. Then the men crept quietly down the mountainside toward the camp of the Midianites.

All the Midianites were asleep. Then Gideon blew his trumpet. The other men blew their trumpets too. What a loud noise it was! Then the men broke their pitchers, and let the lights shine out.

The Midianites woke up and, oh, how frightened they were! "What is happening?" they cried. It looked like a huge army was coming down on them!

The Midianites began running as fast as they could in the darkness. They ran and ran until all of them were gone from the land of Israel.

God had helped Gideon and his brave men save the people from the Midianites. Now the people could go back to their homes. They could gather their own grain for food. They could worship and praise God for His goodness. How glad they were!

Daniel Faces the Lions

Darius, the new king of Babylon, was very glad to have a helper like Daniel. Daniel was a Hebrew who had been captured and carried off to Babylon. He did not worship idols like the people of Babylon did, but worshipped the true God.

"Daniel is so wise and good," the king said, "I will make him the first president in all the land."

When the other rulers heard this, they were jealous of Daniel. "We must watch him and when he does something wrong we will tell the king," they said.

But after they had watched Daniel for a while they gave up. "It's no use," they said, "for Daniel never does anything wrong."

"Wait a minute," said one of them. "I have an idea. Remember how Daniel always prays three times a day to his God? If we could get the king to make a law that no one shall pray to anyone except him for thirty days, we can trap Daniel."

"Let's go to the king at once," they said.

When all the rulers except Daniel stood before the king, they said, "O King, you are so great. Why don't you make a law that no one shall pray to anyone except you for thirty days? If anyone disobeys, he will be thrown into the den of lions."

King Darius thought for a moment. "That sounds good," he said. "If all of you want that law, I will make it."

So the law was written and the king signed it.

As soon as the law was signed, the rulers talked it over among themselves.

"Let's tell Daniel about the new law," they said, "and then see what will happen."

When Daniel heard about the new law, he said nothing to the others. But when it was time to pray, he opened his window and began to pray to God as usual.

The wicked rulers were listening for him. "Now we will tell the king," they said gleefully.

When King Darius heard the news, he was very sad. "Daniel is my best friend," he cried. "I must do something to save him."

All day long the king thought and thought. But there was nothing he could do. The law had to be enforced.

When evening came the rulers said, "Remember, O King, your law can't be changed."

"Bring Daniel to me," the king said sadly.

When Daniel stood before him, the king said, "O Daniel, surely God will help you."

Then Daniel was put into the lions' den. A large stone was put in front with the king's seal upon it.

"What have I done?" cried the poor king. "What have I done?"

"Come, eat your dinner now," said his servants.

But the king could not eat. Neither could he sleep. All night long he paced the floor.

"O Daniel, Daniel!" he cried through the long dark night. At daybreak he ran to the lions' den.

"Daniel, has God taken care of you?" he called out. Then he listened. There was Daniel's voice answering him!

"O King," said Daniel, "God has sent an angel to shut the mouths of the lions. I am not hurt at all."

How happy the king was! "Bring Daniel out of the den at once," he commanded his servants.

When Daniel was out safe and sound, the king made a new law.

"All the people in my kingdom shall fear Daniel's God," he said. "He is the living God and His rule shall never end."

For many years after this Daniel lived as the king's helper and he taught many about God.

A Brave and Beautiful Queen

Everyone who lived in the city of Shushan was very excited.

"The king has sent out word for all the beautiful girls to come to the palace," they said. "He will choose one of them to be queen."

Of course each girl hoped to be chosen. Think how exciting it would be to live in the palace and to wear the royal crown!

One of the men who worked for the king was named Mordecai. He was a Jew who guarded the king's gate. Mordecai had a beautiful cousin named Esther.

"You are beautiful enough to be queen," Mordecai told Esther. "You must go to the palace to see the king."

There were many beautiful girls who went to the palace, but none so beautiful as Esther. When the king saw her, he fell in love with her at once, and chose her to be his queen. So Esther stayed on at the palace.

She wore the beautiful queenly robes and the royal crown.

Mordecai was very happy that Esther was chosen queen.

"Do not tell anyone you are a Jewess," he said.

There was another man who worked for the king whose name was Haman. Haman was very proud and wanted everyone to honor him. As he passed through the king's gate, he wanted Mordecai to bow before him. But Mordecai worshipped God, and did not think it was right to bow before a man.

"Why doesn't Mordecai bow before me?" Haman asked angrily.

"Because he is a Jew," the people told him. "They bow only before God."

"I will ask the king to get rid of all the Jews in this country," Haman said.

Haman went before the king and said, "Do you know there are people called Jews in this country who will not keep your laws? It isn't good to have such people here. If you will sign this paper, I will have them killed—all the men, women, and children."

The king did not know anything about the Jews, but he trusted Haman. Neither he nor Haman knew that beautiful Queen Esther was a Jewess.

"You may do as you wish, Haman," the king said, and he signed the order for the Jews to be killed.

Word went out throughout the country that on a certain day every Jew should be killed. What sad news it was!

Mordecai was greatly distressed when he heard the news. He put on mourning clothes (sackcloth and ashes) and came before the king's gate crying bitterly.

All the other Jews dressed in mourning clothes too and cried loudly.

At last word came to Queen Esther that Mordecai was wearing mourning clothes before the king's gate.

"Oh, he must not do that!" cried Esther. "I will send him some new clothes."

But Mordecai would not wear the new clothes. "Take these back to the queen," he said sadly.

When the clothes came back, Esther knew that something was very wrong.

"Ask Mordecai what is wrong," she told the servants.

Then Mordecai sent word to Esther to tell her all that had happened. He also sent her a copy of the king's message saying that all the Jews must be killed.

"You must go to see the king, Esther, and ask him to save our people," Mordecai sent word.

When Esther heard these words and read the king's order, she was very frightened. Then she sent word back to Mordecai.

"If I go to see the king without an invitation," she said, "unless he holds out the golden sceptre to me, I will be put to death."

Mordecai sent her another message. "You must go and try to save our people," he said. "Perhaps this is why God saw to it that you were chosen queen."

When Esther heard these words she knew what she must do. She sent one more message to Mordecai.

"Have all our people pray and fast for me for three days," she said. "Then I will go to see the king. If I die, I die."

Esther dressed up in her beautiful robes and went to see the king.

What would he do? Would he be angry? Would he have her put to death, or would he reach out the golden sceptre to her? Esther didn't know, but she trusted God to help her.

"Please help me to say the right words, dear God," she prayed.

The king looked up in surprise. Then he reached out the golden sceptre.

38

"What do you want, Queen Esther?" he asked.

"Will you and Haman come to a special dinner I will have for you tomorrow?" she asked.

The king and Haman were very pleased with the queen's invitation.

"We will come," they said.

It was such a wonderful banquet that they accepted Esther's invitation to come again the next night.

When the time for the second dinner came, Esther told the king about the terrible news she had heard.

"I am a Jewess," she said, "and all my people are to be killed by your order."

How surprised and angry the king was! "Who is to blame for this?" he asked.

"Haman is," said Esther bravely.

The king stormed out of the room to stop the order that the Jews were to be killed.

Later Haman himself was put to death, but all the Jews were saved.

"God has heard our prayers," said Queen Esther and Mordecai. "He has helped us to save our people."

And all the people said, "Thank You, God, for brave Queen Esther and Mordecai."

A Little Boy King

What a sad time it was in the land of Israel! The king had died and a wicked queen had taken his place.

"All the king's sons must be killed," said the queen. "None of them must grow up to be king of Israel."

The king's sister Jehosheba heard the cruel words of the queen.

"I must save Baby Joash," she said. Quickly she hid him in a bedroom of the palace with his nurse. Then as soon as she could, Jehosheba slipped out of the palace taking the baby and his nurse with her.

"We will take the baby to the Temple," she whispered to the nurse.

Pit, pat, pit, pat, over the streets they ran as quickly as they could until they came to the Temple.

Jehosheba's husband, Jehoiada, was the minister in the Temple. He was waiting and opened the door for them.

"O Jehoida, we were able to save Baby Joash from being killed."

Jehosheba's hands shook as she opened the blanket to show the baby.

Baby Joash did not look at all afraid. He just smiled and waved his hands in the air.

"We will keep Baby Joash here in the Temple," said Jehoiada. "No one will look for him here."

As the days went by, little Joash was very happy in his Temple home. Jehoiada taught him many things about God. Often they sat together while Jehoiada read to him from a scroll of the Scriptures.

"You must always remember God's laws," Jehoiada would say. "Someday you will be king. You must lead your people to love and serve God."

How exciting all this sounded to Joash!

"I will be a good king," he would say. "I will tell my people to love God. I will tell them to worship here in the Temple. Will you help me to be a good king, Uncle Jehoiada?"

"Yes," Jehoiada would say, "I will help you."

Then one day when Joash was seven years old, Jehoiada came hurrying to find him.

"Come quickly, Joash," he said. "It is time for you to be king."

Jehoida took Joash by the hand and led him out of the Temple. There the people were waiting.

"This is the king's son, Joash," said Jehoiada. "He will be your king now."

Then Jehoiada put a golden crown on Joash' head. He put a scroll in his hand.

"Joash is our king," cried all the people.

Then the trumpets began to blow. The people shouted and praised God.

"Remember the good days here in the Temple," Jehoida said to Joash. "Remember the good things I have taught you about God. I will help you to be a good king."

"I will remember," said Joash.

As long as Jehoiada lived, he helped Joash to be a good king. He loved God and tried to serve Him.

The Still, Small Voice

Elijah, the prophet, stumbled along in the darkness, running as fast as he could go.

"I must hurry," he said, "for the wicked queen Jezebel wants to kill me. She has already done away with all the rest of God's prophets. If she kills me there will be no one left to tell the people about God."

On and on Elijah ran, all that night and all the next day. For forty days and forty nights he traveled until at last he came to a cave on the side of Mount Horeb.

"Oh," cried Elijah, "this looks like a safe hideout. Queen Jezebel will never find me here."

He dropped down on the floor of the cave to rest. How good the cool floor felt to his hot, tired body!

"I need a long, long rest," said Elijah; "then I will decide what to do."

As Elijah lay there resting, he began to think:

"I am all alone," he said sadly. "No one else loves God. No one wants to listen to God's prophets. I might as well not try to preach anymore."

Then suddenly Elijah heard the Lord speaking to him.

"What are you doing here in this cave, Elijah?" God asked.

"Oh," cried Elijah, "I have worked so hard for You, Lord, but look what has happened. Everyone in Israel has forsaken You. They have killed all the other prophets. I am the only one left and now they are trying to kill me."

Elijah did not need to explain all this to God. God knew what had happened to Elijah. God knew something else too. Elijah had not called on God to help him. He needed to learn more about God and to learn to listen for His voice.

"Go out on the mountain and stand before the Lord," God said to Elijah.

Elijah began to feel ashamed that he had not called on God or listened for His voice. He crawled out of the cave as God had said and stood there on the side of the mountain.

As Elijah stood there, he heard the sound of a great wind rushing by. The big rocks all around him began to tumble and fall, and to break into pieces. The trees bent and swayed.

Elijah clung to the side of the cave and listened. Surely God would speak to him in this great wind. But the wind passed by and Elijah did not hear God's voice.

As soon as the wind had quieted down, the earth beneath Elijah's feet began to tremble. The rocks began to shake and tumble down the mountainside. It was a great earthquake.

"Perhaps God will speak to me in the earthquake," thought Elijah.

But when the earthquake was over, Elijah knew that God had not spoken to him.

Listen! Now there was a great crackling sound, and Elisha saw a cloud of smoke rising.

"Look at the fire," Elijah cried and quickly crawled back into the cave for safety.

"Perhaps God is in the fire," thought Elijah. But God did not speak to Elijah in the fire.

"How will God speak to me?" Elijah wondered when the fire had passed.

Then softly, quietly, Elijah heard a whisper, and he knew that God was speaking to him in a still, small voice. Elijah put his robe over his face and stood there in the entrance of the cave, listening.

Then God asked Elijah again, "What are you doing here, Elijah?"

Again Elijah told God why he had run away.

"I am the only one left in Israel who loves You, and they want to kill me," he said.

"You are not alone, Elijah," God told him. "I have seven thousand people in Israel who love Me. Go back to your work and choose a young man named Elisha to help you."

When Elijah heard God's words, he left the cave and went back to his own country. There he found the young man Elisha to help him, just as God had said.

God Talks to the Temple Boy

When Samuel was a little boy, his mother, Hannah, took him to the temple to help the minister, Eli. Eli was an old man and he needed someone to help him. His own sons did not love God. They did not want to serve God, and they did not want to help Eli in the temple. So Eli was very glad to have Samuel help him.

There were many things that Samuel could do to help. Every morning he pushed aside the heavy curtains to let the sunlight in. He dusted the furniture. He polished the golden lamps until they shone. He filled them with oil. At night he drew the curtains together again.

Eli was very kind to Samuel and taught him many things about God. Samuel listened carefully. He wanted to love and serve God. He wanted to be a good helper in the temple.

One night after a busy day in the temple Samuel lay down to sleep on his sleeping mat. He had done many things to help that day and he was very tired. Soon he was fast asleep.

Samuel had not been asleep very long when he heard someone call: "Samuel!"

"Eli is calling me," said Samuel. He ran quickly to see what Eli wanted.

"I did not call you, Samuel," Eli said. "Go back to bed."

Samuel went back to bed but soon the voice called again, "Samuel!"

"Eli did call me this time," said Samuel and he ran back to Eli again.

"I did not call you, Samuel," said Eli.

This happened three times and then Eli said, "God is calling you, Samuel. Go back to bed, and when He calls again, say: 'Speak, Lord; for thy servant heareth.'"

Samuel went back to bed as Eli said. Soon he was fast asleep again. Then suddenly there was the voice again calling, "Samuel!"

This time Samuel did not run to Eli. Instead he answered just as Eli had told him to do: "Speak, Lord; for thy servant heareth."

God had something very important to tell Samuel that night.

"Eli's sons are very wicked," God said to Samuel, "and Eli cannot make them obey. Eli and his sons cannot help my people learn about Me."

As Samuel listened to God, he knew that someday God wanted him to be a minister and teach the people in Eli's place.

All night long Samuel thought about God's words. Suppose Eli should ask him what God had said to him. What could he tell him? Samuel loved Eli and he knew that Eli would be sad to hear what God had said to him. But Samuel also knew that he must do what was right and tell the truth.

When morning came, Eli called Samuel and said, "What did God say to you, Samuel? Do not keep it from me. Tell me all of His words."

Then Samuel told Eli all that God had said to him.

When Eli had heard, he said, "Let God do what seems good to Him."

As Samuel grew up, God was with him. Samuel always did what was good and true, and God helped him.

The Singing Shepherd

"The Lord is my shepherd; I shall not want . . .

"Yea, though I walk through the valley of the shadow of death, I will fear no evil . . ."

These were the words of David, who had once been a shepherd boy tending his father's sheep. Perhaps he had made up the song while he was still a shepherd boy. There were many dangers all around. Hiding behind the rocks and among the bushes and caves were many wild animals. Fierce lions and bears were nearby to harm the sheep and the shepherd must watch them carefully.

Sometimes a bad storm would come. The sky would grow dark, the lightning flash, and the wind howl around the rocks and caves. David would hurry to find shelter for his sheep.

In all these dangers, David was very brave. He thought about how he cared for his sheep, and he knew that God would care for him in the same loving way.

"Surely goodness and mercy shall follow me all the days of my life," sang David.

When David was a shepherd lad he did not know all that would happen in his life, but he knew that God would always be near to him. God chose him to be the future king of Israel.

David became a helper in the palace of King Saul. He was so brave that the king soon made him a captain in the army.

But as time went by, King Saul became very jealous of David. A wicked spirit came into his heart and he wanted to kill David. Once while David was playing his harp for him, the king threw his spear at him in anger.

"I will have to leave the palace at once," thought David, "or the king will kill me."

So David slipped out of the palace and hid from King Saul. For years after this he wandered about without a home. Sometimes he hid in a cave. Always there was danger that King Saul would find him and kill him.

David prayed many times for God to help him. Many times he must have whispered a song to remind himself of God's nearness. God was very near to David and helped him in many ways. There were times when David's friends brought him food and water. They often risked their own lives to warn him about King Saul. Among his closest friends was the king's own son, Jonathan.

After King Saul died, and David became king, there were still many dangers and troubles for David. But he never forgot God's love and care.

One day David was thinking about all the things that had happened to him. He remembered how he had wandered for years without a home, and how he had hid behind the rocks and in caves. But God had been with him. Surely goodness and mercy had followed him all of his life.

Then David sang a new song of praise:

The Lord is my rock . . . in him will I trust . . .
I will call on the Lord, who is worthy to be
*   praised . . .*
In my distress I called upon the Lord, and cried to
*   my God: and he did hear my voice . . .*
Therefore I will give thanks unto thee, O Lord . . .
*   and I will sing praises unto thy name.*

—FROM II SAMUEL 22

The Man Who Believed God

Long, long ago in the country of Uz lived a man named Job. Job was a very rich man. He had many sheep and cattle. He had camels and donkeys. He had servants to help him.

Job was a good man who loved God and tried to please Him. His neighbors worshiped idols, but Job worshiped God. Every day he prayed to God. He prayed that his children would love and serve God also.

Job was a great man and all his neighbors honored him.

"What a good man Job is!" they said. "See how God helps him."

Job often thought about God. He thought about the greatness of God. He thought about the wonderful world that God had made.

"God is very wise and wonderful," thought Job. "Look at the wonders He has made. He made this wonderful world. He made the heavens above. He has done wonders without number. He is so great and good! I will love and serve Him forever."

One day trouble began to come to Job. First some robbers came from another country and stole his sheep, camels, and cattle. His servants were killed. Then a great storm came and Job's children were killed.

Oh, how sad Job was! But that was not the end of his troubles. He became very sick. He had bad sores over all his body. No one wanted to be near him. No one even wanted to look at him. So poor Job left his house and went outdoors. He sat down on a pile of ashes alone.

Some of Job's friends came to see him there.

"Poor Job," they said. "He must have done something very wrong. God is punishing him."

But Job knew better than that. He knew he had done nothing wrong. He knew that God was not punishing him. But he wondered about many things. Why had God let these things happen to him?

"Where is God now?" Job wondered. "I can't find Him. How can I talk to Him and know that He will hear?

"God is so great and so powerful. He moves mountains and overturns them. He spreads out the heavens and makes the waves of the ocean smooth. He made the stars above. Why doesn't He hear me when I am in trouble?"

Job's friends could not tell him the answers. They talked and talked but nothing they said helped Job. His wife could not help him either.

"You might as well die," his wife said. "God does not love you."

But Job did not stop loving God. The more he thought and wondered about God, the more he loved Him, and the more he understood about God.

"All my friends have failed me," said Job, "but I know God is near. I know He lives, and because He lives, I shall live forever with Him."

At last God spoke to Job and asked him some questions. "Where were you, Job, when I made the world?" God said. "Who put the sea in its place? Do you understand about the daytime and darkness? Can you take the stars across the sky? Do you know about the snow and the rain? Can you help the wild things to find their food? Can you tell the eagles how to build their nests?"

Job knew he could not understand these wonderful things. He could only know about them and wonder.

But as he thought about them, it helped to know how great and wonderful God is.

When God had finished talking to Job, Job said, "I can see how great God is. He is greater than I ever thought or knew. I had heard about His greatness but now I know for myself that He loves and cares for me."

God blessed Job and helped him out of all his troubles. And Job's last days were even better than the first. For one thing, he knew more about God. He knew that God was with him no matter what happened. He knew that, of all the wonderful things that God had made, people are the most important. God cares more about people than all the great and wonderful universe. He will be with them in trouble.

II

God So Loved the World

*Stories of Jesus
and His Friends*

A Special Visitor

It was time for Zacharias, the minister, to go down to Jerusalem again. Every year he went there to help with the Temple worship.

"What will you tell the people this year when they come to worship?" His wife, Elisabeth, wanted to know.

"I will remind them of God's promise to send His Son into the world," Zacharias said. "As I go into the holy place to pray, I will ask them to pray outside."

"I wonder when God will send His Son," Elisabeth said.

"Very soon, I hope," said Zacharias. "The world needs a Saviour very, very much. But first God will send someone to tell us His Son is coming and to prepare the way for Him."

"I will pray especially for you this year," Elisabeth said as she told Zacharias good-bye.

Zacharias was thinking about Elisabeth's words as he went down the winding road toward Jerusalem.

"It is good to know that Elisabeth is praying for me," he said. "It is good to know that she is praying for God to send the Messiah into the world. Surely God will send Him before long. Someone will surely come soon to tell us about it."

But Zacharias did not know then what would happen very, very soon.

When Zacharias reached the Temple he put on his special robes and began his work. Each morning he took a dish filled with burning coals from the great altar and went into the holy place to pray alone.

While he was in the holy place praying, the people would stay outside and pray also. Each evening Zacharias did the same thing over again. One morning as Zacarias began to do his work he had a strange feeling in his heart. Surely something unusual was about to happen. What could it be?

He took the burning coals from the altar as usual, and stepped slowly, slowly into the holy place.

"Oh," he cried in surprise, "who is that?"

For there standing in the holy place at the right side of the altar was an angel.

Zacharias was very much afraid. His hands trembled as he held the vessel of burning coals.

Then the angel spoke to him. "Don't be afraid, Zacharias. Your prayers are answered. You and Elisabeth are going to have a son. He shall be great in the sight of the Lord. He shall tell many people of the coming of the Messiah into the world."

Zecharias could hardly believe the wonderful news. "How can I know this? He asked.

"I will give you a sign," the angel said. "You will not be able to speak again until the baby is born."

When Zacharias came out of the holy place, the people wondered what had happened.

"Zacharias must have seen a vision," they said. But Zacharias could not speak a word. He could not talk to Elisabeth either when he reached home. But he wrote out all the good news that the angel had told him.

Then one day the promise came true. Elisabeth and Zacharias had a lovely baby boy. How happy they were! Their neighbors and relatives were happy too.

"His name shall be Zacharias after his father," they said.

"No," said Elisabeth, "his name is John."

"What a strange name!" the people said. "No one in the family is named John. Let's ask Zacharias."

Zacharias couldn't speak but he wrote down these words, "His name shall be called John."

Immediately Zacharias could speak again and he began to praise God for His wonderful promise.

"Blessed be the Lord God!" said Zacharias. "This child shall be the prophet of God."

God's Wonderful Promise

It was a beautiful spring day in Nazareth. Mary sat outside her little home thinking about God. How near and precious He seemed to her on this day!

Then suddenly right before Mary stood an angel. Mary was very much afraid. She had never seen an angel before. Then the angel spoke to her: "Don't be afraid, Mary," he said. "You are greatly blessed of the Lord. He has chosen you to be the mother of His Son, Jesus, who is coming into the world."

Oh, such wonderful news! Mary could hardly believe it. God's people had been looking for such a promised One for many, many years! Now the promise would come true—and she had been chosen to be the mother of God's wonderful Son.

"How can this be?" she asked the angel.

"With God nothing is impossible," the angel said. The angel told Mary more about what was going to happen, and then he went away.

After the angel had gone, Mary thought and thought about the wonderful news. But there were so many things she did not understand, so many things that she wanted to know.

"I must talk to someone," Mary said. "I will go to my cousin Elisabeth's house. She loves God and knows about His promise. She will help me to understand."

So Mary got on a little donkey and started for Elisabeth's house. It was a long way, far up in the hill country. But Mary did not mind. She wanted so much to talk to Elisabeth.

Clip, clop, clip, clop. That was the sound of the little donkey's feet as it went up the winding road.

What a beautiful day it was! The wild flowers were blooming and the birds were singing. Mary's heart was singing too as she rode along.

"Elisabeth will be very surprised to see me," Mary said to herself. "And think how surprised she will be when I tell her about the angel's visit."

Clip, clop, clip, clop.

"Oh, there is Elisabeth's house now."

The little donkey stopped beside the gate and Mary got off. She walked quickly up to the house and knocked at the door. When the door was opened, there stood Elisabeth to welcome her.

"O Elisabeth," cried Mary, "I have come to tell you such wonderful news!"

As soon as Mary spoke, God helped Elisabeth to understand the wonderful news.

"Blessed are you, Mary," Elisabeth said, "for God has chosen you to be the mother of His Son. God will keep His promise because you believe. He will send His Son to be the Saviour of the world."

Mary's heart was so full of joy when she heard Elisabeth's words that she began to sing a beautiful song:

"My soul does praise the Lord . . .

'For he that is mighty hath done to me

great things, and holy is his name.' "

When Elisabeth heard Mary's beautiful song, her heart was full of joy too.

"Stay with me for a while, Mary," she said. "We will talk about God's promise. We will praise Him together."

So Mary stayed with Elisabeth for three whole months. They had many happy times talking about God and His wonderful promise.

Then Mary went back to her own home in the town of Nazareth to wait for the promise to come true.

The Baby in the Manger

The wind went who-o-o-o-o-o very softly over the hills of Bethlehem. It went who-o-o-o-o-o-o around the bushes and over the rocky hillsides. It whispered softly over the sheep that were sleeping there.

The shepherds were watching their sheep through the long night hours. They heard the soft who-o-o-o-o of the wind and drew their robes more closely around them. Then as they watched they talked quietly together.

"What a beautiful night this is!" said one shepherd. "See how brightly the stars are shining. You can see Bethlehem quite clearly."

"Many people are in Bethlehem tonight," said another. "They have come to the city of David to pay their taxes."

"The city of David," said still another shepherd thoughtfully. "That is where the Messiah is to be born someday."

"Not many people remember God's promise now,"

57

the first shepherd said. "Yet I often think about it, and wonder. Will He ever come?"

The shepherds talked on while the wind whispered softly and the stars shone on overhead.

Then suddenly something happened! Something that made the shepherds sit up quickly in wonder and fear! There all around them was a bright light, and an angel stood before them.

"Oh, oh," cried the shepherds, "what is happening?"

"Don't be afraid," said the angel. "I come to bring you good news. 'For unto you is born this day in the city of David a Saviour, which is Christ the Lord. And this shall be a sign unto you; Ye shall find the babe wrapped in swaddling clothes, lying in a manger.' "

And suddenly, there were with the angel many, many heavenly creatures praising God and saying, "Glory to God in the highest, and on earth peace, good will toward men."

Never, never had the shepherds heard such beautiful music. Never, never had they seen such a wonderful sight. What could it all mean?

Soon the music ended and the light faded away. The angels went back to heaven.

Then the shepherds said one to another, "Let us go at once to Bethlehem and see what has happened."

Down the rocky hillsides they hurried as fast as they could go. They walked all the way to the town of Bethlehem. There they found the stable where Mary and Joseph were staying. And there in a manger, sleeping on the hay, was little Baby Jesus.

"This is the Baby the angels told us about," the shepherds said. "This Baby is the Promised One."

Then the shepherds knelt down and worshiped Him. In their hearts was a song of praise to God.

"We must tell others the good news," they said, "for this great joy has come to all the world."

They hurried away from the stable praising God for all they had seen and heard. And they told the good news to everyone they met.

"Christ, the Lord is born in Bethlehem tonight," they said. And all who heard the wonderful news were glad with them.

Wise Men See a Star

Far, far away from Bethlehem some wise men were looking at the sky one night. "Look, look," cried one wise man. "I see a new star in the sky. What does it mean? I wonder."

"I don't know," said another wise man. "But we must find out. Let's see what our books say."

Quickly they opened their books and read all they could about the stars. "This new star means a King is born," they said. "We must follow it and find Him."

"It may be a long, long trip, so we must take plenty of food and water with us."

"We will take gifts too for the new King," they said.

Soon everything was ready for the long trip. There were fine camels to ride on over the sandy desert. There were rich gifts for the new King.

Then the wise men climbed on their camels and started off. Tinkle, tinkle, tinkle, went the bells on the camels' necks. The bright tassels that hung from the camels' bridles waved to and fro.

"We must travel by night so we can follow the star," they said. There it was before them, as bright as it could be.

So night after night the wise men traveled. Day after day they rested. Over the desert trails they journeyed, on and on toward their goal. All the way they followed the bright new star.

At last they reached the city of Jerusalem.

"Where is the new King of the Jews?" they asked.

But no one in Jerusalem had heard about a new king.

"Herod is our king," they said. "Ask him."

But Herod did not know about a new King. "I will ask the teachers in the Temple," he said.

The teachers in the Temple opened God's Book and read what it said about a new King.

"The new King will be born in Bethlehem," they said.

"When you have found the new King come and tell me, so I may worship Him also," Herod said to the wise men.

The wise men turned their camels toward Bethlehem. Now it was night and there was the beautiful star to guide them. They followed it all the way to Bethlehem until they came to the house where Mary and Joseph were staying.

"We have come many, many miles to find the new King," the wise men told Mary and Joseph.

They knelt down to worship Baby Jesus. Then they took out their rich gifts of gold, frankincense, and sweet-smelling myrrh to give to Him.

Before the wise men left to go home, God spoke to them in a dream.

"Do not tell Herod about Baby Jesus," God said, "for he will want to do away with Him."

So the wise men did not go back to Jerusalem. Instead they left for home another way. All the way their hearts were full of joy and praise for Baby Jesus.

Talking in the Temple

Up and down the winding road that led to Jerusalem went Mary, Joseph, and the Boy Jesus. They were on their way to the Temple to worship God.

"I am glad I am old enough to go to the Temple with you this year," said the Boy Jesus happily. "Tell Me more about the Temple, Mother."

Mary had told Jesus about the Temple many times, but now she told Him more as they walked along.

"There are wise teachers in the Temple," she said. "They will tell us more about God."

"I want to talk to the wise teachers," said Jesus. "I want to talk about God."

"Look," said Joseph, "we can see the Temple now. See the beautiful white walls? See the golden roof shining in the sun? We will soon be there."

Many other people were going to the Temple too. Now as they saw it in the distance, everyone began to sing:

> "I was glad when they said unto me,
> Let us go into the house of the Lord."

"We will worship in the Temple," said Joseph. "We will sing and pray. We will give our offering. Then we will be ready to start home again."

But when Mary and Joseph were ready to start home, Jesus was not there to start with them.

"Where is Jesus?" Mary asked.

"He is probably with some of our friends," said Joseph. "We will find Him by nighttime."

But when they stopped for the night, Jesus still was not to be found.

61

"We will have to go back to Jerusalem and find Him," Joseph said.

So Mary and Joseph went back to Jerusalem. They looked and looked but they could not find Him.

"Where can He be?" cried Mary. "We have looked and looked."

"We will keep on looking," said Joseph. So Joseph and Mary searched for three long days trying to find Jesus.

"Let's go to the Temple again," said Joseph. "That is where we last saw Him."

Back to the Temple they went, and sure enough there, sitting among the wise teachers, was the Boy Jesus. He was still talking to them about God.

"O Jesus," said Mary, "we have looked and looked for You!"

"Didn't you know I would be here?" asked Jesus. "This is my Father's business."

"Come home with us now," said Mary.

Jesus was glad to obey and He started on the winding road back home to Nazareth with Mary and Joseph. Jesus was happy to be with His family again, but His mind was filled with wonder at the things He had learned during His visit to the Temple.

The Wilderness Preacher

"Repent, for the kingdom of heaven is at hand." These were the words of John the Baptist as he preached along the banks of the Jordan River.

It was a hard place for a man to preach. The desert sun beat down on his face. The hot winds whistled around the rocks and blew the sand and dust before him. But John did not seem to mind. He kept on preaching his message.

People nearby heard his loud voice and stopped to listen.

"Who is this strange preacher dressed in rough clothing?" they wondered. "Is he a prophet sent from God,"

It had been four hundred years since God had sent a prophet to teach His people.

"Perhaps it is Elijah come back again," the people said. "He is very much like Elijah. He lives out of doors and eats what food he can find. He preaches in a loud voice. Surely this is Elijah."

Soon the word spread into the cities and many people came to hear the strange preacher. As they listened they became sorry for their sins.

"What shall we do?" they asked John.

"Repent and be baptized," John told them.

When the people in Jerusalem heard what was happening, they sent out some priests and other helpers in the Temple to talk to John.

"Who are you?" these men asked him. "Are you God's Son?"

"No," said John.

"Are you Elijah?"

"No," said John. "I am not Elijah."

"Are you another prophet sent from God?"

Again John said, "No."

"Then who are you?" the men asked.

"I am a preacher out here in the desert telling people to repent of their sins and to be baptized," John told them.

"Why do you baptize people if you are not a prophet?"

"I baptize with water," said John, "but Someone is coming soon who will baptize with the Holy Spirit.

He is so wonderful I am not even good enough to untie His shoes."

The men looked at one another. "What can we ask him now?" they wondered. "Surely this strange preacher is speaking God's message."

As days went by, many, many, people came to hear John preach. They listened to his words and repented of their sins.

"We want to be ready when Christ comes," they said. "We want to be baptized."

So day after day John preached to the people out in the desert. He did not seem to mind the heat, the wind, and the sand. He thought only about God's message. Many, many people repented of their sins and were baptized.

Why Jesus Came

"Repent and be baptized; prepare the way of the Lord." These were the words of John the Baptist as he went up and down the land where Jesus lived.

One day when John was baptizing people in the river Jordan, Jesus came to be baptized. Jesus was a grown man now. He was ready to begin the work that God had sent Him to do.

John the Baptist was very surprised when Jesus came asking to be baptized. "You are greater than I," said John. "Shall I baptize *You?*"

"Yes," said Jesus, "for that is the right way."

So John took Jesus down into the river Jordan and baptized Him.

Soon after this Jesus went up north to Galilee preaching to the people. "Repent," He said, "and believe the gospel."

When the Sabbath day came, Jesus went to the synagogue and taught the people there. What wonderful words He spoke! The people wanted to hear every word.

There was a man in the synagogue that day who had an evil spirit. He needed help very much. Jesus felt sorry for the man and healed him. How surprised the people were! Jesus could heal as well as preach. The news spread very fast.

When the service in the synagogue was over that day, Andrew and Peter invited Jesus to go home with them for dinner. They wanted to hear more of His wonderful words. They wanted to be near Him.

When they reached Peter's house, they knew at once that something was wrong.

"Mother is very sick," said Peter's wife. "She has a very high fever."

Then Peter remembered how Jesus had helped the poor man at the synagogue. "Perhaps Jesus can help," Peter said to his wife. So they told Jesus about the sick mother.

"I will help," said Jesus. He went to the mother's room where she lay sick on the bed. He took her hand in His and lifted her up. At once her fever left her. Her sick feeling was all gone.

"I am well enough to help with the dinner," she said happily. She helped Peter's wife to bring out the Sabbath food and place it on the table. How happy and thankful all of them were as they bowed their heads and gave thanks to God!

That evening just at sunset Peter looked out of his house and saw many people coming. They were bringing their sick and crippled friends to see Jesus.

"We need Your help, Jesus," they said.

"I will help you," said Jesus kindly.

He came out of the house and walked among the people. One by one He touched the sick and crippled and healed them. By the time He had healed them all it was very late.

"Stay all night with us and rest," said Peter. So Jesus spent the night at Peter's house. But He did not rest very well. He kept thinking about all the many, many people who needed His help.

Long before daylight Jesus slipped out of the house and went to the country, where He could pray all alone. He needed to talk to God.

When morning came, people began coming to Peter's house again to be healed, but Jesus was not there.

"Where is Jesus?" the people asked. "We need His help very much."

"I will go find Him," said Peter.

Peter hurried out to look for Jesus. At last he found Him where He had gone to pray.

"Many people are looking for You," said Peter.

"I must preach the gospel first of all," said Jesus, "for that is the work that God sent Me to do. Let us go into the next town and preach the gospel there."

Jesus and His friends then went from town to town preaching the gospel. Wherever He went, there were sick people who needed help, and Jesus healed them all.

Jesus Chooses Helpers

All night long Simon and Andrew had been fishing. They had fished and fished but had caught nothing. Now they were washing their nets on the shore.

They were so busy with their work they did not see Jesus coming until He spoke to Simon.

"May I borrow your boat, Simon?" Jesus asked. "I want to sit in it while I talk to the people."

Simon looked up and saw a great crowd of people following Jesus.

"Of course You may use my boat," he said. "Here, get in and I will push it out from the shore for You."

Simon and Andrew both got into the boat with Jesus. Simon rowed out a little way from the shore and then put down an anchor.

Jesus sat in the boat for a long time talking to the people about God. When He had finished talking, He turned to Simon and said, "Row out into the deep water now, Simon, and let down your nets."

"Oh," cried Simon, "Andrew and I have fished all night and haven't caught a fish. But if You say so, we will try again."

Simon and Andrew rowed out into the lake until they came to deep water. Then Jesus said, "Let down your nets, Simon."

Simon and Andrew let down the nets into the water.

Soon Simon cried out, "Oh, our nets are very heavy! Help me bring in the fish, Andrew."

Simon and Andrew pulled and pulled on the heavy nets but they could not bring them in.

"I see James and John over there in their boat,"
said Andrew; "let's call them to come and help us."

Simon and Andrew both put their hands to their
mouths and called out: "Come quickly! We need your
help!"

James and John rowed out as fast as they could
to help Simon and Andrew. Together the four men
pulled and pulled at the heavy nets until they were
brought in. Soon both boats were full of fish.

Simon looked at all the fish. He looked at Jesus, and
then he knew what had happened. It was Jesus' wonderful power that had helped them to catch the fish.

Simon knelt down before Jesus. "Go away from
me, Master," he said, "for I am a sinful man."

"Don't be afraid, Peter," said Jesus. "Follow Me.
From now on you will help Me to win men."

When the boats came to the shore, all four men
left their fishing nets and followed Jesus.

Jesus Goes About
Doing Good

Jesus and His disciples were very, very busy.
They went from place to place, in all the cities and
towns. Jesus taught and preached about God, and
healed the sick, the lame, and the blind.

How glad the people were to have Jesus come!
Quickly the news spread throughout the countryside.

"Have you heard about the wonderful Teacher
called Jesus?" they asked. "He tells about God. He
heals the sick. He helps all who come to Him."

Wherever the good news went the people wanted to see Jesus.

"We want to hear this good Teacher," they said. "We want Him to heal our sick ones too."

All the sick people wanted Jesus to come to their town or city. All the blind people wanted Jesus to come. All the lame, the deaf, and the sad ones wanted Him too.

"Come to our city, Jesus," they cried. "Come and help us."

So Jesus and His disciples kept going from place to place. And everywhere they went great crowds followed them. There were great crowds in the streets of the towns. There were crowds along the country roads.

Some people came running as fast as they could. Some were so sick they had to be carried. The blind and the lame had to be helped along the way.

There were so many, many people that all of them could not get near to Jesus. They bumped into one another. Some of them fell down and cried out for help. Some of the sick ones fainted along the way. Oh, how much the people needed help!

Jesus was so sorry for the people who crowded around Him. "So many people need to be helped," Jesus said. "There are not enough workers to take care of them all."

Then Jesus said to His disciples, "Pray that God will send more helpers."

The disciples saw how much Jesus loved everyone, and how He wanted to help all who came to Him. More and more they understood why Jesus came into the world. They were glad too that Jesus had called them to be His disciples.

The Man Who Came at Night

Nicodemus opened the door of his house one night and looked out.

"It is dark now," he said to himself. "No one will see me if I go now."

Nicodemus was one of the rulers of Jerusalem. He was an important man.

Quietly he closed the door behind him and started down the dark street. His sandals made a soft swishing sound on the rough stone streets as he walked along.

"I must see Jesus," Nicodemus said to himself. "I know He is a Teacher from God, but some people do not think so. I want to talk to Him alone."

Nicodemus walked on and on through the dark streets until he came to the house where Jesus was staying. He went *knock, knock, knock,* at the door. A friend of Jesus opened the door at once.

"May I speak to Jesus?" asked Nicodemus.

"Yes, He is in the guest room on the roof," the friend said.

So Nicodemus went up the stairs to the room on the roof. There was Jesus resting quietly after a long day of work.

"Sit down, Nicodemus," said Jesus. He did not seem surprised to see this important man.

The stars were shining overhead. The wind was blowing gently through the leaves of the trees nearby.

"Jesus, I know You are a Teacher from God," said

Nicodemus. "I know God helps You do all these wonderful things."

Jesus listened to Nicodemus and then He said, "Nicodemus, you must be born again."

Nicodemus was a very wise man, but he could not understand what Jesus meant. Jesus was trying to tell him that he should stop his old way of living and to start a new life with God.

"I don't know what You are saying," he said.

"Do you hear the wind in the trees, Nicodemus? You can't tell where it comes from or where it goes, but you know it is there."

"Yes," said Nicodemus.

"I am telling you what I know about God. You must believe what I say even though you do not understand it," said Jesus.

"God loved everyone so much that He gave His own Son. Whosoever believes in the Son will not be lost but will live forever. God sent His Son into the world that all who believe in Him might be saved."

Nicodemus listened to the wonderful words of Jesus. He could not understand them, but now he knew that Jesus was more than a Teacher sent from God. Jesus was God's own Son.

As Nicodemus walked slowly back home, he thought of all that Jesus had said. Why, this was something wonderful! Jesus, God's Son, had come into the world. Whosoever believed in Him would have eternal life. That meant to live forever with God.

"Whosoever means me too," said Nicodemus. "Now I believe that Jesus is the Son of God. I will follow Him."

The Little Lost Sheep

When Jesus taught the people about God, He often told stories to help them understand. When He talked to farmers, he talked about sowing seed. When He talked to fishermen, He talked about catching fish. He taught in a way that people could best understand.

One day when Jesus was teaching, many of the people listening were shepherds. Jesus talked about good shepherds and how they care for their sheep. Then He told them a story.

There was once a good shepherd who had a hundred sheep. Every night the sheep were put into a sheepfold. There they were kept safe from the wild animals and the storms.

Every morning the shepherd would open the door of the sheepfold and let the sheep out. He would lead them out on the hillsides and through the valleys. He knew just where to find the sweet, tender grass for them to eat and the cool, sparkling water for them to drink.

In the heat of the day he would lead them to a shady place to rest. Sometimes when a little lamb was too small to keep up with the others, he would carry it lovingly in his arms.

When evening came, the shepherd always led his sheep back to the sheepfold. If any were cut or bruised from the rocks and bushes, he poured oil on their wounds. And always the shepherd counted his sheep to be sure than none was missing.

One night a shepherd was counting his sheep as they went through the gate.

"One, two, three . . ." On and on he counted until he came to "ninety-five, ninety-six, ninety-seven, ninety-eight, ninety-nine." That was all! One of his sheep was missing!

The shepherd knew at once what he must do. He locked the gate to the sheepfold and started out to find the missing one.

The shepherd forgot how tired and hungry he was. He thought only about the poor little sheep lost somewhere among the rocks and thorns. He must hurry, for darkness was coming fast. Soon the wild animals would be out looking for food. A sheep would be just what they were after!

Among the rocks and cliffs he went, calling, calling.

"Ta-a-a-a-a-a-a, ho-o-o-o-o-o-o," he called over and over again. Surely the sheep would hear his voice and answer him.

At last up among the steep cliffs he heard a tiny "Baaa-a-a-a-a," very faint and far away. Quickly he climbed up until at last he found the lost sheep. It had fallen behind a steep rock, and there it was, waiting for help to come.

The shepherd took the poor little sheep in his arms and started back to the sheepfold. How happy he was that he had found his sheep! And how glad the little sheep was when at last he was safely in the fold with the others!

Then the shepherd called to his friends and said, "Rejoice with me; for I have found my sheep which was lost."

When Jesus had finished His story about the lost sheep, the people who were listening knew more about God. They knew that God is like a good shepherd and that He loves everyone. He cares when we are lonely and afraid. He is always ready to help us. When someone does wrong things and feels very far away from God, God wants to help and to forgive.

"There is joy in heaven," said Jesus, "when someone comes to God and asks forgiveness for his sins."

"I Can See!"

Tap, tap, tap, went the blind man's cane as he walked along the road one day. Then *tap, tap, tap,* went his cane against the trunk of a big tree.

"Here is my tree," he said. "I will sit in the shade and beg as the people pass by. Perhaps some of them will give me some money."

The blind man sat down beneath the tree and pulled his ragged clothes around him. Then he reached out and touched the trunk of the tree with his fingertips.

"I wonder what a tree really looks like," he said sadly. "I can feel the bark in my fingertips. I can hear the leaves stirring in the wind, but I can't see it like other people say they can. I wonder what the sky looks like, too, and the grass along the road. I hear people talking about these things but I will never know what they look like. I will always be blind."

Whenever the blind man heard people walking along the road, he held out his hands and said, "Will you please help me?"

Some of the people stopped to drop money into his hands. Others passed on by.

Then Jesus and his disciples came along. The blind man heard the *pat, pat, pat* of their sandals and the sound of their voices as they talked together.

"Help me," he cried and held out his hands.

Jesus stopped beside the man. "I will help you,"

74

He said, but He did not give him money. Instead, He stooped over and mixed a little clay from the dust of the road. Then He put the clay on the man's eyes.

"Go wash your eyes in the Pool of Siloam," said Jesus.

That seemed like a strange thing to do, but the man did not ask why. Instead he picked up his cane and started walking down the road as fast as he could. Even though he was blind he knew how to find the Pool of Siloam.

Tap, tap, tap, went his cane before him until at last he came to the pool. *Tap, tap, tap,* went his cane around the edge of the pool.

Then carefully he knelt down and washed his eyes. As he washed away the clay, something wonderful happened. Suddenly he could see! He could see the sparkling water of the pool. He could see the blue sky overhead.

"Oh, I can see!" he cried. "I do not need my cane anymore. I do not need to sit and beg!"

How beautiful everything looked to him as he walked along!

"I can see! I can see!" he cried to everyone he met.

Then the man thought, "I want to see Jesus. I heard His voice and felt His kind hands, but I want to see His face."

The man did not know where to find Jesus, but Jesus knew where to find him. He came and stood beside him. How glad the man was to see His kind face and loving smile!

"Do you believe on the Son of God?" asked Jesus.

"Who is He?" asked the man.

"You have *seen* Him and talked to Him," said Jesus.

Then the man knew that Jesus was God's Son. "Lord, I believe," he said, and knelt down to say, "Thank You," to Him.

When Jesus Came Late

Lazarus tossed to and fro on his bed. "Oh," he cried, "my head, my head! And I am so hot and thirsty. Will you bring me another drink of water?"

"Yes," said his sister Mary, "of course I will." Quickly she held a cup of water to Lazarus' dry lips.

Martha stood beside the bed too, looking sadly at Lazarus.

"Let me rub your head, Lazarus," she said. Gently she rubbed his aching forehead.

"If only Jesus would come!" sighed Mary. He would make our brother well."

"Perhaps He will come today," said Martha.

Mary and Martha did everything they could for Lazarus. And all day long they kept watching the road to see if Jesus was coming. But when nighttime came, Jesus was not there.

"Lazarus is very, very sick tonight," Martha whispered to Mary. "He may not live until morning."

"Oh," cried Mary again, "why doesn't Jesus come?"

All night long Mary and Martha stayed beside Lazarus. They held his hands and bathed his hot brow. But before morning came, Lazarus died.

Mary and Martha were very sad, for they loved their brother very much.

Kind friends heard the sad news and came to help them. Tenderly they wrapped Lazarus' body in linen cloth and carried him away to a tomb.

Mary and Martha walked sadly along and watched as Lazarus was put in the dark tomb. Then they went sadly home again.

"Why didn't Jesus come when we needed Him?" they wondered.

Four days went by. Mary and Martha stayed in their home weeping. Friends tried to comfort them but there was little they could do.

Then suddenly someone said, "Jesus is coming!"

When Martha heard these words she hurried out of the house and ran down the road to meet Jesus.

"O Jesus," she cried, "if you had been here my brother would not have died."

"Your brother will live again, Martha," said Jesus. Then he asked, "Where is Mary?

"I will send her to you," said Martha. She went back to the house and whispered to Mary, "Jesus wants to see you."

Mary arose quickly and went to the place where Jesus was waiting.

"O Jesus," said Mary, "if You had been here, my brother would not have died!"

When Jesus saw Mary and all her friends weeping, He began to weep too.

"Show Me where Lazarus is buried," He said.

So Mary, Martha, and their friends went to Lazarus' tomb.

"Open the tomb," Jesus told them.

When the tomb was open, Jesus prayed to God, and then He called out, "Lazarus, come out."

There was a sudden stir in the tomb, and then Lazarus came out.

"Take away his burial clothes," said Jesus.

Oh, how happy Mary and Martha were! Lazarus was alive again!

"Thank You, Jesus," they said, "for raising our brother from the dead."

How surprised all the people were at the wonderful thing that had happened!

"Surely Jesus is the Son of God," they said to one another.

Then Mary and Martha said to Jesus, "Come to our home with us, Jesus. We will have a good meal together. We will have a happy time thanking and praising God."

A Father Asks for Help

Once there was a rich man who lived in the city of Capernaum. He had a fine home and servants to work for him. He had a little boy he loved very much.

"What a happy man I am!" he thought.

But one day his little boy became very, very sick.

"Oh, oh," cried the little boy, "my head hurts so much! I am so sick!"

"What can I do for my little boy?" the worried father said to himself.

The servants brought water for the little boy to drink. They put cool cloths on his head and rubbed his hands gently. But the little boy grew worse.

"I must have help for my little boy," the poor father said.

Then someone told him some good news. "Jesus is not far away. Perhaps He will come to Capernaum and heal your little boy."

"I will go at once and find Jesus," said the father.

He got on his fastest horse and went down the road to find Jesus. *Clippety clop, clippety clop,* went the horse's feet.

The man rode and rode until at last he came to the place where Jesus was. The man quickly got off his horse and went to Jesus.

"Jesus," he said, "will You come to Capernaum and heal my little boy? He is so sick he is about to die."

Jesus looked kindly at the anxious father.

"You may go back home," he said. "Your little boy will live."

How happy the father was to hear these words! "Thank You, thank You, Jesus," he said.

He got back on his horse and went home as fast as he could go. *Clippety clop, clippety clop,* back to Capernaum he galloped.

When he got near to his home his servants came out to meet him.

"Your little boy is well," they said.

And, oh, there was the little boy, standing in the doorway, waving to his father!

The glad father jumped off his horse and ran to the house. He stooped down and hugged his little boy very tightly.

"When did this happen?" he asked his servants.

"Yesterday, about the seventh hour," the servants said.

"That is just the time Jesus told me he would be well," the father said.

Then the father and everyone in his house said a thank-you prayer to God.

A Sudden Storm

Jesus was very, very tired. All day long He had been helping people. Now it was nighttime and He needed a good rest.

"You are so tired, Jesus," said His disciples. "You must have rest."

"Yes," said Jesus. "Let us go across the lake."

"Come into the boat with us," they said. "We will row You across the lake."

Jesus got into the boat and went to the back where He could lie down.

"Here is a good pillow for Your head," His disciples said.

"Thank you," said Jesus. Soon He was fast asleep.

While Jesus slept, the disciples talked quietly together.

"Look how dark the sky is tonight," said one. "I am afraid it is going to storm before we reach the other side of the lake."

"The wind is beginning to blow now," said another.

The wind blew harder and harder. It stirred up the water on the lake until the waves were very high.

"Look at the big waves," said the frightened men. "Soon they will go over the top of our boat."

Just then a big wave of water did splash into the boat.

"Oh," cried the men, "another wave like that and the boat will sink and we will all drown. Why doesn't Jesus wake up?

"Wake up, wake up, Jesus," they cried. "See the bad storm? Hear the wind and the waves? The boat is getting full of water. Don't You care if we all drown?"

Jesus opened His eyes and looked around. He saw the dark sky overhead. He saw the great waves tossing the boat. He heard the wind howling.

Jesus stood up and spoke to the wind and to the waves. "Be still," He said to them.

Then something wonderful happened. Suddenly the wind stopped blowing, the waves stopped beating against the boat.

Jesus looked at His frightened disciples and said, "Why were you afraid? Don't you have faith in Me?"

The disciples looked at one another in great surprise. "How wonderful Jesus is!" they said. "Even the wind and the waves obey Him. We should never be afraid when He is with us."

Helping a Man in Trouble

One day when Jesus was teaching the people He said, "Thou shalt love thy neighbour as thyself."

A lawyer who was listening wanted to ask a question. "Who is my neighbour?" he asked.

"I will tell you a story before I answer," said Jesus. This is the story Jesus told.

One day a man took a trip from Jerusalem to Jericho. It was a lonely road which wound through rocky hills. Along the way some thieves jumped out and stopped him. They took all his money and his clothes. Then they beat him and left him lying by the side of the road.

The poor man lay there for a while not knowing what to do.

"I shall surely die unless someone comes to help me," he groaned.

The man began to call, "Help, help, help," in a weak voice. Would anyone come to help him?

Not many people passed that way but he kept calling. He was cold and, oh, how he ached and hurt from the cruel beating!

"Help, help," he called again, and listened. Then he heard something! Someone was coming. He raised his aching head a little and saw a priest from the Temple coming.

"Oh," said the man, "perhaps the priest will help me."

The priest came nearer and saw the man lying beside the road.

"Robbers have been here," he said. "They may still be hiding behind the rocks or bushes. I must hurry. I can't stop to help anyone."

"Please help me," said the poor man, but the priest pretended not to hear. He hurried down the road as fast as he could go.

The poor man dropped his aching head down on the ground again. He was disappointed but he did not give up. Surely someone would come to help him soon. In a little while he heard footsteps again. He raised his head to look.

"Here comes a Levite," he said. "He helps the priest in the Temple. He will help me. Help, help, help," he called as loudly as he could.

But the Levite looked at the poor man and shook his head. "I don't know this man," he said. "He is not one of my friends. I can't take time to help him. I must do my work at the Temple."

So the Levite went on the other side of the road and pretended not to see him.

The poor man was growing weaker now. He lay very still by the side of the road. He could not live very long unless someone helped him.

In a little while he heard something else. *Clip, clop, clip, clop,* came the sound of a donkey's feet along the rocky road. Slowly, painfully, the man lifted his head a little. There was a man riding on the little donkey.

This man was a Samaritan. The Jews usually would not have anything to do with the Samaritans, for they disliked them.

"He will not help me," said the man sadly. "He will not even stop."

But the Samaritan did stop as soon as he saw the man lying by the side of the road. He quickly got off his donkey and knelt down beside the wounded man.

"Poor man," he said kindly. "You are badly hurt. But I will help you."

He took some medicine and put it on the man's cuts and bruises. Very carefully he wrapped the injured places and eased the pain as much as he could. Then he carefully lifted the man on his donkey and started down the road. Soon they came to an inn where they could stay all night.

The man was put into a good, comfortable bed. There he was cared for during the night.

When morning came, the man was better but he was not able to travel yet. The Samaritan needed to go on his trip. He could not stay any longer. But before he left he gave the inkeeper some money. Then he said, "Will you take care of this man until he is well? If this is not enough money, I will give you more when I come back."

The Samaritan told his friend good-bye and went on his way. He had done everything he could to help someone in need.

When Jesus had finished telling the story, He asked the lawyer a question: "Which of the men who saw the poor man needing help was a real neighbor to him?"

"The man who showed kindness," said the lawyer.

"Then you go and show kindness to others also," said Jesus.

A Little Boy Helps Jesus

One day a little boy was walking along by the Sea of Galilee. It was a beautiful day with the blue water of the lake sparkling in the sunlight.

"I will get to see Jesus today," the little boy said to himself. "I will stay all day too. I am glad I brought my lunch."

What a good lunch it was too! There were freshly baked bread and two little fish. Just the right amount for a hungry boy, and, oh, it smelled so good!

Soon the little boy saw a great crowd of people up ahead. Jesus was walking up a hill and many people were following Him.

"I will follow too," said the little boy.

Up, up, up the long hill went Jesus. Up, up, up went the crowd of people, with the little boy following along.

Jesus sat down on the side of the hill and began to tell the people about God.

The little boy slipped through the crowd until he was near enough to see Jesus and hear His words.

"God loves you very much," Jesus was saying. "He wants to help you."

"I am glad to know that God loves me," the little boy thought to himself.

He stayed there in the crowd all day, listening to Jesus. He was so busy listening and watching everything that he even forgot to eat his lunch.

As the day wore on, Jesus said to His disciples "What will all these people eat for dinner?"

The disciples shook their heads. "We don't have any food," they said, and it would take a lot of money to buy it in town.

The little boy heard these words. He walked up to one of the disciples named Andrew, and said, "I will give my lunch to Jesus."

"Thank you," said Andrew. He took the lunch to Jesus.

"Here is a little boy's lunch," he said, "but what is that among so many people?"

Jesus took the lunch and said, "Tell the people to sit down."

Then Jesus bowed His head and prayed, "Thank You, Heavenly Father, for this food."

He began to break the bread and fish into small pieces, and His disciples passed them out to the people. Soon everyone had some bread and fish to eat, and there was some left over.

"Gather up the food that is left," said Jesus. The disciples gathered up twelve baskets of food that was left over.

The little boy watched in amazement. Jesus had done something wonderful. He had taken his small lunch and had used it to feed all these people. There had been a lot left over.

"I'm glad Jesus let me help," he said softly.

Jesus Rides into Jerusalem

Once a year the Jewish people held the Feast of the Passover. This was to remind them of the time God had helped their forefathers escape from the land of Egypt. Many, many people went to Jerusalem for this great event. Jesus and His disciples went every year.

On one of these trips, as they came near to Jerusalem, Jesus said to two of His disciples, "Go into the next town and you will find a colt tied up there. Bring it to Me."

The two disciples went as quickly as they could and brought the colt to Jesus. Then they spread their coats on the colt's back and helped Jesus up to ride on it.

When other followers saw what was happening, they spread their coats in the road for the colt to walk on.

"Jesus is riding into Jerusalem like a king," they cried.

The crowds of people along the way became very excited. "Jesus is going to be our King," they began to shout.

They broke branches off the palm trees and waved them in the air.

The children saw what was happening and they became excited too. They picked beautiful flowers and tossed them into the road ahead of Jesus.

"Jesus is our King," they shouted.

There were many, many people in the crowd that day who knew and loved Jesus. There were men, women, boys, and girls whom Jesus had helped.

"This is Jesus, who raised Lazarus from the dead," the people shouted.

"This is Jesus, who healed my blind eyes," cried one man.

"Jesus made my little boy well," said another.

"This wonderful Jesus healed our sick and helped our blind to see," shouted the people.

"Hosanna! Blessed is He that cometh in the name of the Lord."

Jesus rode into Jerusalem on the little colt. The great crowd of people followed along, shouting praises and waving palm branches. What a wonderful day it was!

But some of the people did not praise Jesus that day. Some of them did not want Him to be their King.

"Tell these people to keep still," they said angrily to Jesus. "It is not right to sing praises to You this way."

But Jesus did not tell the people to keep still. He was glad to hear their praises. He knew that in a few days He would die for their sins and for the sins of the whole world.

"If these people did not praise Me, the stones along the road would cry out," said Jesus quietly.

So the people kept on singing praises to Jesus. They followed Him all the way to the Temple, shouting, "Hosanna! Blessed is He that cometh in the name of the Lord!"

Jesus Gives His Life

The light from the small oil lamps flickered and cast strange shadows on the walls of the room. Jesus and His disciples were in this quiet place upstairs eating the Passover supper together.

As they sat there in the dim light, Jesus looked lovingly at His friends. Then He said gently, "I wanted to have this last supper with you before I die."

The disciples looked sadly at one another. Jesus had told them that He must die on the Cross.

"I must suffer many things before the elders and chief priests," He had said, "and then I will be put to death. On the third day I will rise again."

Was this the time when all these things would happen? The disciples could hardly believe it.

Jesus turned to Judas and said, "What you are going to do, do quickly."

Judas got up from the table and hurried out into the darkness of the night.

The other disciples did not think it strange when Judas left the room. Their hearts were too sad over the news that Jesus had just told them.

When the meal was over, Jesus led His disciples down the stairs and out into the street.

What a strange night it was in Jerusalem! There seemed to be a feeling in the air that something dreadful was about to happen.

Many people had come to Jerusalem for the Passover, but Jesus and His disciples did not go near the crowds. Instead they slipped quietly through the dark streets and out the city gate to a garden at the foot of the Mount of Olives.

Just inside the garden, Jesus stopped. "Wait here," He said to eight of His disciples. "Peter, you and James and John come with Me."

Deeper into the shadows of the old olive trees went Jesus with His three disciples. Then He said, "Stay here and watch while I pray."

Jesus went a little farther into the garden. He dropped on His knees and began to pray: "O My Father, take this cup from Me if it be possible; nevertheless, not My will but Thine be done."

As Jesus prayed there in the garden, angels came and helped Him. Soon He arose and went to His disciples.

"Let us go now," He said quietly.

The disciples had not watched as Jesus had asked them to do. Instead they had fallen asleep. Now they arose quickly and rubbed their eyes to see what was happening.

Suddenly they heard the sound of angry voices. A mob was coming, and the men were carrying clubs and torches. In the flickering light of the torches the disciples saw the wicked face of Judas! He was leading the soldiers right to Jesus.

"Oh, how could Judas do such a terrible thing!" they wondered. But Jesus was not surprised. He knew why Judas had left the supper that night.

Now the soldiers took hold of Jesus and led Him away. The angry mob followed along, cursing and shouting angry words at Jesus.

The disciples were very frightened. All of them ran into the darkness as fast as they could—all except Peter and John, who followed along well behind the crowd.

What a terrible night followed! Jesus was taken first before the elders and priests, as He had said he would. Then He was taken before Pilate, the Roman governor. The angry mob began to shout, "Crucify Him! Crucify Him!"

Finally Pilate said, "Take Him and crucify Him if you will. But I can find no fault in Him."

Then Jesus was severely beaten and a crown of thorns was placed on His head. The soldiers spit on Him and called Him evil names, but Jesus answered not a word.

Later that morning, Jesus was led along the narrow streets of Jerusalem, and beyond the gate to a hill called Calvary. There He was nailed to the Cross and hung between two thieves.

While Jesus was there on the Cross, He prayed for those who had so cruelly treated Him, "Father, forgive them; for they know not what they do."

This was the saddest day in all the world. The sun disappeared and the sky grew dark. Finally Jesus said, "Father, into Thy hands I give My spirit," and He died. There on the Cross that day Jesus, the Son of God, died for the sins of the whole world.

The earth began to tremble and shake, and a great earthquake followed. What a terrible time it was!

When the people saw these things happen, they said, "Surely Jesus was the Son of God."

The friends of Jesus came and took His body. Among them were Nicodemus and a rich man named Joseph. Lovingly they wrapped His body in linen and put sweet spices around it. Then they laid Him in a new tomb and rolled a big stone in front of the door.

The women who had sadly stayed beside the Cross that day now watched to see where His body was laid.

"We will come again after the Sabbath," they said, "and bring sweet spices to show our love for Him."

Then all the friends of Jesus went sadly away.

The Tomb Is Empty

It was very early in the morning after the Sabbath when Mary, the mother of James, Salome, and Mary Magdalene started toward the tomb where Jesus was buried.

"All night long I have been thinking," said Mary sadly. "How can we roll away the heavy stone from His grave?"

"We should have asked Peter to come with us," said Salome. "He is big and strong."

"We have not seen Peter since Jesus was crucified," said Mary Magdalene, "but perhaps the guards will help us."

"We must anoint the body of Jesus," said Mary. "It is all we can do for Him now."

"Let's walk faster," said Salome. "See the streaks of light in the sky? Soon the sun will rise."

"Here is the garden now," said Mary Magdalene. "And, oh, look! The stone has been rolled away!"

"What has happened?" cried Mary. "Have they taken His body away?"

"Yes, I am afraid so," said Mary Magdalene. "I must run and tell Peter what has happened."

Mary ran quickly through the quiet streets until she came to the house where Peter was staying. She pounded on the door and Peter opened it. He looked as though he had not slept all night long.

"O Peter," cried Mary Magdalene, "Come quickly. The stone has been rolled away from the tomb. We think the Lord's body has been taken away!"

"John is here too," Peter said. "We will come at once."

The three of them started back toward the garden as fast as they could go. John ran ahead and reached the tomb first. He stooped down and looked into the grave.

When Peter came running up, he went right into the tomb.

"Yes, His body is gone," he said sadly. "I can't understand what has happened."

Very sadly he and John started home again. But Mary Magdalene did not leave.

"I wonder where Mary and Salome are," she said to herself. She did not know that an angel had spoken to them and had told them some wonderful news.

Mary Magdalene sat down beside the tomb and wept. Then suddenly she heard a voice saying, "Why are you weeping?"

Mary thought it was the man who took care of the garden.

"Sir, if you have taken away Jesus' body, tell me where it is," she said without looking up.

Then something amazing happened! Mary heard Jesus speak her name, "Mary," and looking up she saw Him standing beside her.

"O Master!" she cried joyfully.

"Go tell My friends I have risen from the dead," Jesus told her.

Then Mary's happy feet fairly flew over the cobbled streets back to find Peter.

"Peter, Peter," she cried, "John, and all the rest, I have seen Him, I have seen Jesus! He is alive! He is risen from the dead, and sent me to tell you!"

"Oh, how can this be?" cried the disciples. "We must see Him for ourselves."

"You will," said Mary happily. "He is alive; He is alive, and you will see Him again."

Walking and Talking with Jesus

Along the road to Emmaus walked two friends of Jesus. They were not going very fast. They were talking together and looked puzzled and sad.

"I wonder if it is really true," one of them said. "I don't see how it could happen."

"I don't know," said the other one, "but the women say it is true. They saw the empty tomb. They heard the angel say that Jesus had risen from the dead."

"Peter and John looked in the tomb," said the first friend. "They said it was empty."

The other friend shook his head. "It is all very strange," he said. "I wish I knew for sure. I wish we could see Jesus ourselves and then we would know."

The friends were so busy with their thoughts that they did not at first see that someone else was walking beside them. At last this person spoke to them.

"What are these things you are talking about?" he asked. "And why are you so sad?"

Then one of Jesus' friends whose name was Cleopas said, "Are you a stranger around here? Don't you know all the things that have happened lately?"

"What things?" asked the one who walked beside them.

"Well, about Jesus of Nazareth. He was a great Prophet sent from God. He did many wonderful things and spoke many wonderful words. But the chief priests and the rulers put Him to death on the Cross. We could hardly believe it! We thought He was going to be our King!

"But now the strangest part of all! Today some of the women who were friends of Jesus went to the tomb about dawn. They had taken spices and perfumes for His body. But it was not there! The tomb was empty. An angel was there and he said that Jesus had risen from the dead. 'Go and tell the others,' the angel said.

"Then some of the men ran to see the tomb. It really was empty. But they didn't see Jesus."

"We do not know what to believe now," said the other friend.

Then the person who had suddenly appeared to them said, "Oh, can't you believe what the prophets have said? This was the Christ, who suffered these things. He has risen from the dead."

Then He began to explain the Bible and tell why Jesus had come into the world. How carefully the friends listened! What a wonderful story it was!

At last the three of them came to Emmaus.

"I must leave you now," said the one who walked with them.

"Oh, no!" cried the men. "Stay and eat dinner with us. We want to hear more about the Christ."

As they sat down to eat together, this friend took bread in his hands and broke it. Then he thanked God. There was something familiar about it!

"Oh," cried Cleopas, "You are Jesus!"

It really was Jesus, their wonderful Friend. He had walked with them and talked with them. But suddenly He disappeared.

Cleopas and the other friend looked at one another. "Did not our hearts feel warm and happy when Jesus was with us?" they said. "We must hurry back to the city and tell the others."

94

They went back to Jerusalem as fast as they could go.

"Jesus has risen indeed! We have seen Him. We have talked with Him," they told the friends in Jerusalem.

The friends were very glad to hear the good news. But they too wanted to see Jesus and talk with Him.

Do You Love Me?

It was evening on the Sea of Galilee. The sun was going down, making a golden path across the water.

Peter sat in his boat near the shore. Thomas, Nathanael, and other disciples of Jesus were standing on the shore.

"I am going fishing," said Peter.

"We will go with you," said the other disciples.

So all the disciples climbed into Peter's boat and started out across the water. When they came to the deep water they let down their nets.

As the disciples fished, they talked about all the things that had happened in Jerusalem.

"Jesus is really alive," said Peter. "We have seen Him and talked with Him."

"Yes," said Thomas, "it was hard for me to believe at first, but now I know it."

"I wonder when we will see Him again," said Nathanael. The disciples fished on through the long night hours, but they did not catch any fish. Every time they lifted the nets, they were empty.

Soon streaks of light showed in the sky and the shadows began to disappear.

"The sun is coming up," said Peter. "We might as well go in now."

The disciples lifted their nets and started for the shore.

As they drew near the shore one of them said, "Look, someone is standing there on the shore."

Then a voice called out across the water, "Have you caught any fish?"

"No," answered the disciples.

"Then cast your net on the right side of the boat."

The disciples cast their net on the right side of the boat, and what do you think happened? Soon the net was so full of fish they could not draw it in.

"O Peter," said John, "it is the Lord speaking to us."

Peter was so excited he jumped right into the water. He wanted to get to Jesus as fast as he could.

When Peter came to the shore, there was Jesus waiting for him. Jesus had made a nice fire and had breakfast all ready for them.

Soon the disciples and Jesus sat down together around the warm fire to eat breakfast. How wonderful it was to be with Jesus, their kind, loving Friend!

When breakfast was over, Jesus said to Peter, "Peter, do you love Me?"

"Yes," said Peter, "You know I love You."

"Feed My lambs," said Jesus.

Three times Jesus asked Peter if he loved Him. Three times He told Peter to feed His lambs and sheep.

Peter knew what Jesus meant. He knew that Jesus called himself a Good Shepherd. The sheep were all the people who needed to hear about God's love. Jesus wanted Peter to tell people the good news.

Peter could not know all that Jesus meant. But he knew one thing. He loved Jesus enough to do whatever Jesus wanted him to do.

He Will Come Again

After Jesus had risen from the dead, He stayed with His disciples for a while. For forty days He met with them and told them many more things about God and His kingdom.

"Go into all the world and tell the good news," Jesus told His disciples. "Tell the people to repent and be baptized. Tell them to keep all the commandments I have given you. I will be with you always, even unto the end of the world."

Then one day as Jesus talked to His disciples, He led them out toward the Mount of Olives. This was a mountain close to Jerusalem.

As they came up on the mount, Jesus spoke to His disciples for the last time.

"Stay in Jerusalem until the Holy Spirit comes to you," He said.

Then the disciples asked Him, "Lord, when will You start Your kingdom on this earth?"

"It is not for you to know this," said Jesus. "Only God knows the right time for His kingdom to start. But when the Holy Spirit comes, He will give you power to do the work I have given you to do.

"You shall be My witnesses in Jerusalem, in Judea, and in Samaria, and to the uttermost parts of the earth."

When Jesus had spoken these words, He began to rise from the ground and up toward the sky. Up, up, up, He went, with the disciples watching Him. Oh, what was happening? They were so filled with wonder they could not say a word. Then Jesus disappeared into the clouds and was gone from their sight. Oh, how they wondered! They stood there watching and watching. Would Jesus come back again soon?

While they were still watching, two angels dressed all in white stood beside them.

"Why are you standing here looking up into heaven?" the angels said. "This same Jesus which was taken from you shall come again in the same way as you have seen Him go."

Then the disciples stopped looking up in the sky.

"Jesus has gone," they said, "but He will come again someday. Let us go to Jerusalem now and wait for the Holy Spirit to come."

They turned and started down the mountain toward Jerusalem. Although Jesus was gone, they were not sad now. Their hearts were full of joy and praise as they thought of all that had happened.

"We will obey His commandments," they said. "We will look for Him to come again someday. What a wonderful day that will be!"

The Blinding Light

After the Holy Spirit had come upon them, friends of Jesus started out at once to tell about Him. As Jesus had told them to do, they started first in Jerusalem and the countries round about. Many people were glad to hear about Jesus. They believed on Him and were baptized. The new church began to grow very fast.

But then trouble came in Jerusalem. Some people

were not glad to hear about Jesus. They did everything they could to stop His friends from telling the good news. One of these was a young man named Saul, who thought he was doing God's work by opposing Jesus' friends.

"We must not let this new religion spread," Saul said to his friends. "We must go to every house in Jerusalem and find all those who say they are followers of Jesus. We must put them in jail, so they cannot tell about Him anymore."

So Saul and his friends went up and down the streets finding all those who loved Jesus. Many of them were put in jail and others had to run away for their lives. But everywhere they went they told about Jesus.

When the news reached Saul that people in other cities were being told about Jesus, he was very angry. He was especially angry when he heard the news had reached as far as the city of Damascus. Quickly he went to the rulers of Jerusalem.

"If you will give me letters to the governor of Damascus," he said, "I will go there and arrest any who are friends of Jesus. It doesn't matter if they are men or women, we will bind them up and bring them back here to be put in jail."

"You may go," said the rulers. And they gave Saul the letters he needed.

Soon Saul and his helpers were on the way to Damascus to arrest the friends of Jesus there. Day after day they traveled along the dusty road. Saul was not very happy as he went along. He kept thinking about the brave followers of Jesus who had been treated so cruelly in Jerusalem. He remembered especially one young man named Stephen who had been stoned to death. How brave he had been and how kind and forgiving to the very end! Saul had stood by and watched this happen. He could not forget it. Surely Stephen did not deserve to die like this!

"I must not think about these things," Saul told himself. "I am going to Damascus to arrest other friends of Jesus. Some of *them* may even need to be stoned to death!"

When Saul and his friends were almost to Damascus, something strange happened! A bright light shone all around Saul. He was so surprised and so blinded by the light that he fell to the ground. Then he heard a voice speaking to him, "Saul, Saul, why are you working against Me?"

"Oh," cried Saul, "who are You?"

"I am Jesus," the voice answered. "It is hard for you to fight against Me."

Saul began to tremble all over and he was still blinded by the light. "What shall I do, Lord?" he asked.

"Stand up," Jesus told him, "and go on to Damascus. There you will be told what to do."

Saul stood up but he could not see which way to go, as he was now blind.

"We will help you," his friends said. They had seen the light and had heard the voice but did not understand what had happened.

"Take me to Damascus," said Saul.

Saul was in Damascus three days and three nights without being able to see. He could not eat or sleep. He was so sorry for all the wrong things he had done!

Then a friend of Jesus, named Ananias, came to see him.

"Brother Saul," said Ananias, "the Lord Jesus has sent me to help you receive your sight and to receive the Holy Spirit. He has chosen you as a very special worker for Him."

At once Saul could see again.

How wonderful it was! Saul, who later was called Paul, had found the Lord Jesus as Saviour. His sins were forgiven and the Holy Spirit came into his heart. Then he was baptized as a believer.

From now on he would be *helping* to tell people about Jesus, not fighting against Him. Because of his preaching and writing many people would hear about Jesus and would receive Him as Lord and Saviour.

Preaching by the Riverside

"Lord, help me to go to the right cities to tell the good news about Jesus." This was Paul's prayer over and over again as he and his friends traveled about preaching the gospel. There were so many places to go. Paul wanted to be sure the Holy Spirit was leading as he went from place to place.

One night as Paul was sleeping, he had a dream. In this dream he saw a man who said, "Come over to our country and help us." When Paul awakened, the Holy Spirit helped him to know this dream meant to go across the sea to the land of Macedonia.

So Paul and his friends took a ship bound for Macedonia. They came first to the beautiful city of Philippi, where few people had ever heard of God, and none had ever heard of Jesus.

When the Sabbath day came, Paul wanted to go to a synagogue to worship.

"Where is your synagogue?" he asked the people.

"We don't have a synagogue in Philippi," he was told. "Only a few women meet together to worship on the Sabbath day."

"Where do they meet?" Paul asked.

"Down by the river," was the answer. "One of them is a woman named Lydia. She is a fine woman who loves God."

"We will find these women and worship with them," said Paul.

So Paul and his friends went outside the city of Philippi and walked down the road toward the river. There beneath a big tree sat a few women and children.

It was a beautiful place to worship. The wind whispered softly through the leaves of the trees. The sunlight sparkled on the river that ran past.

"May we worship with you?" Paul asked.

The women were very surprised to see Paul and his friends, but they were glad to have someone else worship with them.

"Of course you may," said Lydia kindly.

The men sat down under the big tree. Paul began to preach a sermon.

"You have met here to worship God," he said. "I want to tell you about Jesus, God's Son, who came to be your Saviour."

Then Paul told how Jesus had come into the world and how He had suffered and died for their sins. He told how Jesus had risen from the dead on the third day and had appeared to His friends. Then he told how Jesus had gone back to heaven to be with God.

"Jesus wants to be your Saviour too," said Paul. "That is why we have come to Philippi to tell you about Him."

All the women listened very carefully to what Paul had to say. When he had finished, Lydia said, "I believe on the Lord Jesus. I want to be baptized at once."

"You may," said Paul.

So Lydia and other members of her family were baptized at once in the river. How happy Lydia was to know that her sins were forgiven, and to know that now she belonged to Jesus! But she wanted other people in Philippi to know about Jesus too.

"Please come to my house to stay while you are in Philippi," she said to Paul.

So Paul and his friends went to Lydia's house to stay. While they were in Philippi, many people heard the gospel and became Christians. Soon there was a good church in Philippi, and it helped to spread the good news to others.